AF515982

Beethoven
AND FRIENDS

Beethoven AND FRIENDS

Kishore Chatterjee

NIYOGI
BOOKS

Published by

NIYOGI
BOOKS

D-78, Okhla Industrial Area, Phase-I
New Delhi-110 020, INDIA

Tel: 91-11-26816301, 26813350, 51, 52
Fax: 91-11-26810483, 26813830

email: niyogibooks@gmail.com
website: www.niyogibooks.com

Design: Navidita Thapa/Niyogi Books

ISBN: 978-81-89738-49-5

Year of Publication: 2009

Printed at: Niyogi Offset Pvt. Ltd., New Delhi, India

In memory of the Renaissance
and early music connoisseur,
the late Pratap Narsingh Rao,
who opened the window for me
into the fascinating universe
of medieval and Renaissance music.

Contents

Author's note

greatest gift I have received from the Almighty is my ability to love Western classical music. Good music is for sharing, and in my own way—through lectures and the written word, educational films and painting exhibitions, I have tried to share this love I have felt for the Bach tribe with the people of India.

That is why when in 1997 *The Statesman* offered me a fortnightly column on the composers and their world, I jumped at it. I felt it would enable me to bring in more friends for Beethoven, Bach, Mozart and the rest. The column has now been running for eleven years. It was originally called 'Classical Gas'. Then in the new century, the title was changed to 'Strings Attached'. In it I have covered the life and times of the composers, the music forms, stories about classical music, and much more. For a long time, I have been receiving requests for a book based on the column. With the help of Niyogi Books, that wish has now been fulfilled.

This book includes among others, a selection of articles that have appeared in the column and aims to talk to those who are attracted by Western classical music and want to know more about the composers and their world.

The aim is to enthuse, excite and make the reader more curious to listen to music that is one of the greatest treasures of mankind.

I owe a special word of thanks to many people.

Michael Flannery of *The Statesman* for suggesting the idea of the column in the first place. Soumitra Das for introducing me to Niyogi Books, which set the ball rolling; Dipa Chaudhuri for being so understanding in the editing stage; Navidita Thapa for the lovely design; Debojoy Chanda for the initial typing and selection; Indranil Poddar for all his suggestions; my wife, Maitreyi, for building up a regular clipping service over the years to help me with information; Chitro Sen, Anirudh Chari and Shauri Bannerjee for obtaining information from various sources. And above all, *The Statesman,* for believing that Western classical music has takers in India.

Marble bust of Bernard Shaw by A. Rodin, one of the music critics the author greatly respects.

Finally, my thanks are due to all my readers who wanted the book. Here it is at last.

My love affair with Western classical music began very early; at the age of thirteen, when I entered the Doon School. There I met two Parsee boys, both older than me, who loved music and were avid music collectors. Till then, all the music that I knew was the songs of Rabindranath Tagore whose music resonated in my family all the time. My father also sang Verdi's 'La donna-e-mo-bi-le' and talked about Caruso and Toscanini. But they were just names to me without any musical significance. I was not prepared for the kind of music that I was now about to hear.

The younger of the two boys regularly received parcels of records. I remember they were huge orange labelled and red labelled 78 rpm records, which he brought out from brown paper sleeves with pictures of opera singers. To me they were very strange-looking people with weird dresses. I used to watch fascinated. We shared the same room in Kashmir House and I think my lifelong love for records and recordings started there, in Dehra Dun, in 1951. The older boy, Sheel, would play the records on the common room radiogram. I was too scared to talk to him but every time I could get away, I would go to hear the music. To say I was bowled over would be putting it mildly. I had never heard anything quite like it. I do not think any other music I ever heard made quite such an impact. Decades later, I realized that the music he played most often and which remained buried in my memory was Rimsky Korzakov's *Scheherazade* and Beethoven's *Moonlight* Sonata. The second movement of *Scheherazade* haunted me for years until one day, while sitting in a record shop, I identified it. The melody of my childhood returned to me and my search was over. But my quest for the secrets of classical music was just beginning.

The year was 1960. I had a job and all my money went in collecting classical records. I could not afford sound equipment, so I went to people who had a radiogram and took my small collection of records with me. I began with the Beethoven Violin Concerto, some Chopin, the *Moonlight* Sonata of Beethoven, Mozart's *Jupiter* and G Minor symphony and Bach's Violin Concertos. That was all I could afford. For the first ten years of my collecting life I did not think of communicating my joy of listening to classical music. But deep within me, I felt that I was very lucky that I could listen to Mozart, Haydn, Bach, Beethoven, Schubert, Brahms—the lot. I was convinced that this was one of the abiding glories of mankind, as vital as the sculptures of Michelangelo, the paintings of Leonardo da Vinci and the plays of Shakespeare.

I began to read about music. The more I read, the more curious I became about symphonies and concertos and the lives of the composers. Then in 1970, during the Beethoven birth bicentenary, All India Radio, Calcutta, invited me to give an hour-long talk on Beethoven and his deafness. This was the first time I talked about why I loved classical music. After that, I became a regular broadcaster over the radio on Western classical music. At that time there was a slot late at night for special programmes.

Apart from individual composers I did a series on 'Who's Afraid of the Bach Tribe?' This was my first

Record collecting has been a passion with the author.

attempt to popularize the classics which was to become my passion and obsession. This was followed by the world of opera and a series on great music critics—Robert Schumann, Ernest Newman, Edward Hanslick, Bernard Shaw, Donald Francis Tovey and Neville Cardus—the six greatest music writers of all time. Secretly, I had decided that I was going to write and talk about the world of Beethoven and friends whenever and wherever I got an opportunity. Then a door opened: I read a book called *The Golden Road, A Record Collector's Guide to Classical Music* by Harvey Blanks, who was the editor of the World Record Club in Australia. I wrote a letter to him saying how difficult it was for Bach and Beethoven lovers to collect records in India (as it was at that time). Harvey responded immediately by sending me more than twenty LP records which included Handel and Vivaldi; two composers almost non-existent at that time in India. I considered this a miracle, a gift from the composers. Harvey and I became friends and we started a correspondence through which Harvey talked about music and shared his love for the classics with me. In the early seventies there was no e-mail, no internet and no computers. Our letters took time. Sometimes they got lost. He continued to send me records, enriched my collection and changed my life. I realized the value and joy of sharing music and decided to dedicate myself to this task.

The arrival of the Long Playing Records from Australia was not without adventure. I was paranoid about the Indian Post Office and my pet nightmare those days was that my records were either being stolen or lost. The bad dreams were not without reason.

At one time, the records arrived looking like boats. Harvey was an expert at packing LPs, it was his job as the World Record Club coordinator, but the Indian Post Office had opened the package, and without knowing what it should do with records by Corrette, Tartini, Locatelli and Haydn, they actually hid the LPs, and all my enquiries yielded a short answer 'hasn't arrived'. When I finally got the LPs, the records were beyond playing. Then Harvey, very patiently, taught me how to straighten the LPs with solar energy and two glass sheets. I finally managed. Another time, the post office and the customs called me a gold smuggler and I had to appear in court. What happened was this—Harvey had sent me the complete Ring Cycle by Wagner with Solti conducting the Vienna Philharmonic, recordings that have now been designated through extensive voting as the 'Recording of the Millennium'. Wagner's *Ring* is often referred to as *The Golden Ring* and Harvey had written on the packet *The Golden Ring*. Neither the post office nor the customs authorities would believe that I was not trying to smuggle gold. It took all my ingenuity to convince the people at the court that it was classical music and not caskets of gold.

Western classical records have never been freely available in India. During the 78 rpm era which launched my career, the records in those huge brown sleeves, used to come from abroad and the collectors had to be satisfied with what they got unless they had a source to get stocks from abroad. Then came the Extended Play (very brief) and Long Playing (Monophonic) era when the Gramophone Company (sometimes known as HMV or EMI) began to manufacture them in India. They had a very small catalogue, but it did comprise fabulous performances and great recordings; today in the CD era they are all collector's items and reference recordings: Otto Klemperer's Beethoven symphonies, Curzon playing the Beethoven concertos, recordings by Thomas Beecham and Rudolf Kempe, Claudio Arrau's early recordings of the Beethoven sonatas, to mention just a few. The stereo era that followed in the late sixties followed the same policy. They were wonderful recordings, great performances, but they were very few. Then came what I call the 'Russian Years' with Melodiya recordings which widened the repertoire and coincided with the arrival of a few performances on cassettes. The Melodiya records made us savour some great recordings by the Russian interpreters like David Oistrakh, Svyatoslav Richter, Emil Gilels and Mstislav Rostropovich. But it was a brief interlude that moved into the CD era when Western classical recordings on labels other than HMV-EMI became available. Today a young person beginning a collection has a much better choice and more outlets of availability than I had when I began in the late fifties. From the mid-seventies, I began to write about music in *The Statesman*. It was around that time that I paid a brief visit to the UK and Europe to attend concerts and meet great musical personalities and to talk over the BBC on the problems of record collecting in India, a problem that still exists because the Indian market for Western classical recordings has always adopted a 'take it or leave it' policy. This makes it almost impossible for the buyer to get the desired music and collecting becomes so difficult and adventurous. Some of the most precious recordings in my collection have come from the second-hand market.

By the time I came to write my *Statesman* column 'Classical Gas' in 1997, I had been talking about music regularly and searching for ways to win more friends for Beethoven and Bach. Three years after the column started, I wrote a play called *Clara* on the lives of Schumann, his wife Clara and Brahms. The play was produced by Max Mueller Bhavan with Zarin Choudhury, a well-known theatre personality, in the role of Clara. I mention this because I want to underline my search for communication channels which continues even today. *Beethoven and Friends* is the result.

In 1997, my Listener's Club, which had been running for years in Max Mueller Bhavan, moved to The Calcutta School of Music. The club is a collection of people who love classical music and their repeated request has given me the idea to put my writings on Western Classical music together. In the year 2000, I held an exhibition on Beethoven which explained through paintings the story of the composer's life, his tragedy and triumph. Around this time came my four short films: *Symphony, Beethoven, Vocal Music* and *Mozart* for the University Grants Commission. Then in 2003, the *Statesman* column changed its title from 'Classical Gas' to 'Strings Attached'. But my quest to win more friends for the Bach tribe continues. If you are reading this book, don't be afraid of classical music—it will give you a great deal of joy and fun.

Kishore Chatterjee, Calcutta, 2009

Chapter 1

Power & Glory

Beethoven the Colossus

In the world of Western classical music, think of classical music and pat comes the name, Beethoven. What gives Ludwig van (1770-1827) this special place? As Leonard Bernstein asked long ago in his famous essay on the composer: 'Why Beethoven?'

One lifetime is not enough to unravel the mysteries of this composer but a lifetime of listening does reveal certain clues. This composer who was a god to all who came after him—Schubert, Mendelssohn, Schumann, Brahms, Wagner, to mention just a few—like Shakespeare, da Vinci and Michelangelo appeals at once to the connoisseurs and the masses. This sets him in a class apart.

After all, think of a composer becoming deaf. Therein lies the key to Beethoven. It was the cause of all his agony, trauma and trials. It is also the reason why his music is so pure, so unique, so different. Beethoven has left detailed documents of what becoming deaf meant to him—in letters and in conversation books, which had to be used to communicate with him. But none is more moving than the *The Heiligenstadt Testament,* a piece of prose as profound as Oscar Wilde's *De Profundis*. Deafness also made Beethoven's music develop spiritually. For him, music became an expression of the conquest of tragedy and every new piece of music Beethoven wrote while coping with his tragedy was more profound and more significant than the previous opus. This progression makes him totally different from all other composers.

There is hardly a single dull bar in Beethoven although his early music is less important than his later music. He wrote very little compared to Bach, Handel, Mozart or Haydn—about 136 works and some posthumous discoveries. The cliché 'quality and not quantity', is what the Beethoven's world is all about. Basically, nine symphonies, five piano, one violin and one triple concerto, thirty-two piano sonatas, some sixteen string quartets, one opera, a few violin and cello sonatas, a few songs and some overtures and incidental music is all that he offers to the world. Yet, in

Bust of Beethoven by Franz Klein.

them is a depth of beauty and philosophy, a worldview that has few equals in music or in other arts.

Remembering Beethoven is also a unique experience. He has no melodies conventionally speaking, but sound patterns that hit the mind. He gives you little that you can whistle in the bath. Yet he draws you in with the first bar and holds you enthralled till the last. There is hardly a single popular tune in Beethoven except perhaps *Für Elise,* now used for calling bells. Yet his music, is so simple, so enchanting and so romantically intense that you return to it again and again. This incredible drawing power is what makes Beethoven so popular. Examples are the Third, Fifth and Ninth symphonies. The beginning of all three hits you. Yet try to find the melody and you'll spend a lifetime searching. You can't ignore Beethoven. From the first bar he holds you spellbound.

Beethoven is the most rugged and masculine of composers. Yet, the slow movements, the adagios, and the largos of his sonatas and symphonies involve you emotionally, completely. He is like a king weeping and this is one of the secrets of his appeal. Take the slow movement of the Sonata *Pathetique*, the allegretto of the Seventh Symphony or the beginning of the *Moonlight* Sonata, there is music here that automatically makes you bury your head in your hands. Yet try to analyze what it is that appeals and you might as well try and paraphrase the beauty of a sunset.

Beethoven is truly beyond words. That is why all words that have been written about him, all the books, biographies and essays are not a substitute for listening to his music. Ultimately, there is his music. Fortunately, most of Beethoven's music is available in India. Look for it. Life can offer fewer pleasures more rewarding.

THE MAGIC OF NINE

any music has magic, it is in Beethoven's nine symphonies. The supernatural touch that Hector Berlioz and Franz Liszt tried to blend into their compositions came naturally to Beethoven. It has something to do with the number nine perhaps. Beethoven died without completing more than nine symphonies. After his death, composers like Anton Bruckner, Johannes Brahms and Gustav Mahler built a myth around Beethoven's symphonic oeuvre.

Soon word got around that it was not possible to write more than nine symphonies in a lifetime. Bruckner died without even completing his ninth which has three movements, the fourth usually filled up by his *Te Deum*. Mahler, the sensitive soul that he was, became paranoid about writing symphonies. When it came to his ninth symphonic opus, he decided not to call it a symphony at all. It became a song cycle—*The Song of the Earth*—which was actually a symphony for two voices and an orchestra. He called his next symphony, a purely instrumental work, his *Ninth*, hoping to escape the jinx. But Mahler died soon after, leaving an incomplete Tenth.

If some composers have been haunted by the thought of Beethoven completing just nine symphonies, others like Brahms became obsessed with the very act of writing symphonies after Beethoven. Brahms felt that Beethoven had raised the stature of the symphony to such a level that it was not possible to compose symphonies any longer without his shadow looming on the score. The result was that, Brahms destroyed his symphonies until, finally in 1876, at the age of forty, he published his first symphony in C Minor. But the jinx did not leave Brahms. Critics in Vienna described the symphony as the Tenth, implying that it was in fact Beethoven's Tenth symphony being completed at last by another composer. Brahms never really got over his Beethoven complex. But not all composers have reacted to Beethoven's nine symphonies either as musical black magic or as a stumbling block towards original creativity. Indeed, another and more positive reaction resulted as Beethoven did take the symphony to levels that no other composers had done before. It made composers after him discover new symphonic continents. The way was shown by Berlioz through his *Symphonie Fantastique* and taken up by Liszt in his two symphonies—*Dante* and *Faust*.

Thus, it was Beethoven who really gave birth to the 'Romantic' symphony, which reached an apotheosis in works such as Vaughan Williams' *Sinfonia Antarctica* and Gorecki's Symphony no. 3 almost 200 years after Beethoven.

Before Beethoven arrived on the scene, the symphony belonged to Haydn and Mozart. Official records say that Haydn wrote 104 symphonies, but some scholars believe that the number may be more. Until the other day, we all believed that Mozart wrote 41 symphonies, but there may be more.

But why did Mozart and Haydn write so many symphonies and Beethoven only nine? The answer lies in the changing equation between the composer and society. Mozart and Haydn wrote symphonies because they were commissioned and paid for composing. Beethoven composed symphonies because the compulsion came from within. With him began the era of the individual artist. In terms of personal angst resulting in creative compulsion, Beethoven and the Beatles are on the same plane. Beethoven was the first modern composer.

And he was never more modern than in his symphonies. Take the introduction of the First Symphony, the work that launches the whole mighty cycle. It is best described perhaps as a twang, akin to unleashing a musical arrow. Nothing like this introduction exists in the whole of the Classical Age. However, the rest of the symphony is a fairly straightforward work, a delight and a joy forever. The Second Symphony has the first of Beethoven's meditative slow movements and the whole work can be said to have been structured round it. Just as the umbilical cord connects the newborn to it's mother, the first two of Beethoven's nine symphonies are, in spirit, connected with the world of Mozart and Haydn. Beethoven cuts the umbilical cord with the fabulous *Eroica*. This is one of the most discussed and talked about symphonies in existence. His Third Symphony, *Eroica,* is an angry, tempestuous work. Beethoven was angry with his hero Napoleon for having declared himself emperor. He destroyed the original dedication, changed the title from *Napoleon* to *Eroica* and killed his lost hero with a funeral march. The first two movements of the *Eroica* hold the key to this awe-inspiring work and in the third movement Beethoven launched yet another of his innovations—the scherzo, a bit like the Mozartian minuet gone wild. It is this movement that comes back again and again through all subsequent symphonies from Bruckner to Shostakovich.

Even Beethoven enthusiasts tend to neglect the Fourth Symphony. It is like a lost valley between two giant peaks, the *Eroica* and the *Fate*. While I don't agree with the conductor, Thomas Beecham, that it is

A quotation from Beethoven.

the only real symphony that Beethoven composed, it has an incredibly beautiful introduction which Beethoven compared to the early morning light and a slow movement that is simply ravishing. The Fifth Symphony, *Fate,* is probably the most famous of them all with its 'knock on the door' and the *Pastoral,* his Sixth Symphony, is the quintessence of romanticism with its nature programme. Many believe it is his most religious work. The Seventh Symphony made the composer Weber declare that Beethoven was 'now ready for the madhouse', while the short Eighth Symphony is music's greatest epigram. But it is *Choral,* the Ninth Symphony with its fabulous choral ending that probably changed the course of symphonic music. This is where Mass music and classical music meet. Like da Vinci's *The Last Supper,* it is a milestone in the history of civilization.

"I am all that is.
I am all that is, was and ever shall be.
No mortal has lifted my veil.
He alone is of Himself, and to Him alone
All things owe their origin."

Beethoven's sketch for Ode to Joy *from the Ninth Symphony.*

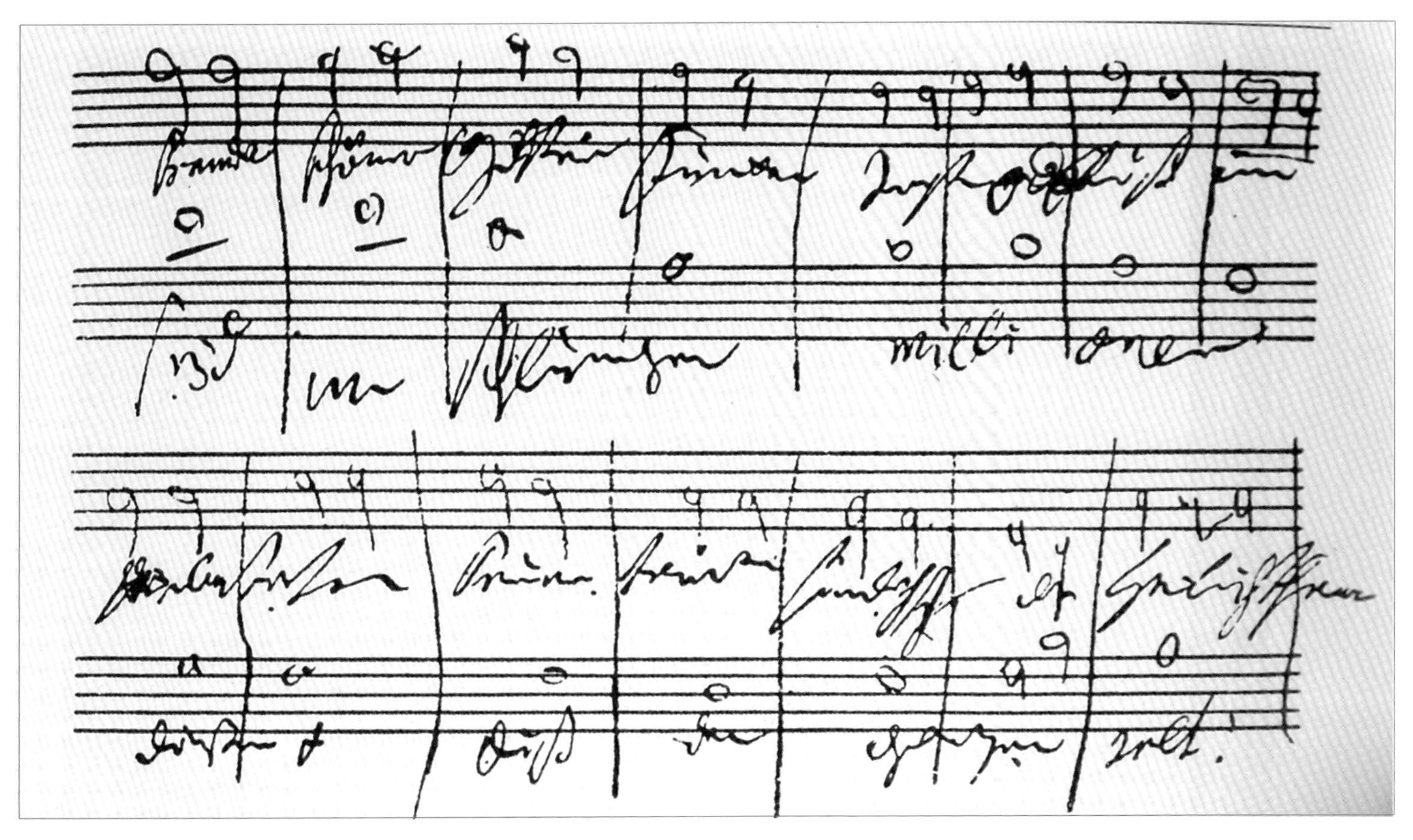

Deafness was Beethoven's greatest tragedy. This is the kind of ear trumpet he used.

RAY AND BEETHOVEN

Just as the cycle of nature renews itself with the arrival of new seasons and the New Year, so does the Beethoven symphonic cycle retain that element of freshness and surprise to generations of new listeners. I am always delighted to meet a person who has never heard a Beethoven symphony before. For, with the first hearing, he or she will perform a musical miracle—start a love affair that will last a lifetime. Just like it happened with the great Indian film-maker, Satyajit Ray. He told me how in his student days, he came in contact with the Beethoven symphonies through 78 rpm records. Being a student, he did not have enough money to buy a complete symphony, so he took home one movement at a time (remember that in the 78 rpm days, a Beethoven symphony would spread across many sides and several discs). Ray became familiar with the symphonies movement by movement, and began to love them. A time came when he felt that they were some of the world's most precious creative treasures and no sensitive human being should be without them. So much so that he worked out a way of judging human beings by asking them if they liked Beethoven's symphonies. If the answer was positive only then would he probe further and ask if they were 'odd' or 'even' beings—if they preferred the 'odd' numbered symphonies (1, 3, 5, 7 and 9) or the 'even' numbered ones (2, 4, 6 and 8)—trying to figure out how he should behave with them on the basis of this information. In his attitude towards Beethoven and particularly his symphonies, Ray was no exception. Throughout the world, there are many Beethoven-crazy people. There are performers, interpreters, conductors, collectors and listeners all over the world for whom Beethoven will remain the ultimate listening experience, a miracle of life and nature like the rain, the stars, the moon and the sun.

The Great Testament

32 piano sonatas by Beethoven represent a pinnacle of achievement in the history of Western music. They make a wonderful autobiography that tells you a lot about Beethoven the man, his philosophy and attitude to life, and his spiritual development.

The piano was the true voice of the Romantic Age and Beethoven was the first of the Romantics to speak completely and comprehensively about life and death through the piano. He understood the piano for he was himself a brilliant pianist who took Vienna by storm as a young man. Although Haydn and Mozart before him had written many piano sonatas, Beethoven extended its scope, and gave the piano sonata epic proportions, heightened drama and seriousness. While his symphonies are more popular and his concertos perhaps more easily approachable, the piano sonatas hold the key to the man that was Beethoven. Without a close knowledge of these sonatas, the heart of Beethoven cannot be reached.

Beethoven composed his piano sonatas in groups and it is easy to remember them if you think of the opus numbers, like op. 2 representing three early sonatas and op. 10 also representing three sonatas. To make the total canvas clear, I shall first segregate the isolated sonatas. These are:

Sonata in E flat, op. 7 (an exquisite work)
Sonata no. 8, op. 13, *Pathetique* (very famous and justly so)
Sonata no. 26, op. 81a, *Les Adieux* (a strange and tantalizing work)
Sonata no. 27, op. 90 (utterly scintillating)

All the other sonatas either come in pairs, or as a trilogy, or in clusters. Those that have common opus numbers like the op. 31 trilogy or the op. 27 or op. 49 duos are easier to identify than the clusters. There are two broad clusters. I call them the 'twenties' and the 'hundred' clusters.

Beethoven published a series of magnificent sonatas as his 'twenties' opus. They are:

Sonata no. 11, in B Major op. 22
(perhaps the most classical of all his sonatas)
Sonata no. 12, in A op. 26 (with the great funeral march)
The two op. 27 sonatas which include the world famous *Moonlight* Sonata
Sonata no. 15, in D Major, op. 28, *Pastorale*

The 'hundred' cluster known as the 'late' sonatas and composed in Beethoven's last years, are:

Sonata in A, op. 101 (music like a garland of stars)
Sonata in B flat Major, op. 106, *Hammerklavier* (contains the greatest slow movement Beethoven ever composed)
Sonata in E Major, op. 109 (perhaps the finest nocturne ever composed)
Sonata in A flat Major, op. 110 (music's final word)
Sonata in C Minor, op. 111 (a postscript to the final word)

Let us now look at the sonatas that share a common home or opus. The first of these is the op. 2 trilogy followed by the op. 10 trilogy. All the sonatas, particularly the op. 10 works, have deeply meditative slow movements and suggest that from an early age, Beethoven was a thinker and a philosopher. The two op. 14 sonatas are, however light-hearted, as are the two little sonatinas that Beethoven published as op. 49. But the three op. 31 sonatas are full of storm and stress, and tempestuous passions. They are vehicles for virtuoso pianists to show their technique and flair, but as a group they contain some of Beethoven's most lofty and grand music.

The 'fifties' trilogy—op. 53, op. 54 and op. 57—contain two of Beethoven's greatest and most oft-played sonatas—the *Waldstein* (op. 53) and the *Appassionata* (op. 57). The little op. 54 sonata is a special favourite of mine and contains music that is similar in mood to the other two. The op. 90 sonata can be described as a harlequin transforming himself into a butterfly. It is like quicksilver, shifting like the mist. Two other sonatas must engage our attention. They are the 'seventies' duo, op. 78 and 79—the sonatas in F sharp Major and G Major—utterly fascinating music which Beethoven composed in the evening of his life looking back on it with a sad, wistful smile.

More than his symphonies, Beethoven's piano sonatas and string quartets reveal facets of the man behind the musician. Studying the 32 piano sonatas is akin to reading a novel like *The Brothers Karamazov* or *War and Peace*. It is an epic of life and death.

Having located the milestones among Beethoven's piano sonatas, we must decide which are recommended listening, assuming that we may get an opportunity to listen to all the sonatas. There are very few people with any claim to interest in Western classical music who have not heard the *Moonlight, Pathetique, Waldstein* and *Appassionata* sonatas. I shall assume these as heard melodies, but in Beethoven's world of sonatas, those unheard are even sweeter. You can skip the first three sonatas, though they are delightful, and go straight to the E flat, op. 7 for its profound depth and many-splendoured dimensions. Listen also

Beethoven nears the end, wild as the west wind. Study by Batt.

Death mask of Beethoven by Franz Klein.

to op. 10, no. 3 which has one of the greatest slow movements Beethoven ever composed, and then move to op. 26 with its funeral march. It is this movement that most influenced Chopin and Liszt and all the Romantics. You will love the fabulous *Pastorale,* and for sheer drama, there are very few pieces of music in Beethoven to match his op. 31, no. 2 *(Tempest)*.

Two of his 'seventies' sonatas—op. 78 and op. 79, are the quintessence of classical music. Listen to the two-movement sonatas, op. 54 and op. 90. Sooner or later, on the journey through classical music you must come to terms with Beethoven's *Hammerklavier*. It is the Mount Everest of music and requires some effort to scale initially, but the mental energy spent is worth it. For in the adagio sostenuto movement, Beethoven wrote in musical terms the equivalent of all the meditations that the science of yoga teaches us. Late at night when the world sleeps, listen to this music, and you'll reach a level of spiritual ecstasy that is probably what the Greeks meant by *catharsis*.

This great sonata will open the gates towards the house called 'Late Beethoven'. There Beethoven lives with his last piano sonatas and the late string quartets. And I recommend you visit this house regularly. If you can't afford all the late sonatas, get the last two, op. 110 and op. 111, which usually come together.

Almost all the great pianists have played Beethoven since the middle of the last century, but the most perceptive Beethoven pianists who have recorded his sonatas are Wilhelm Kempff, Solomon, Wilhelm Backhaus, Claudio Arrau and Claudio Schnabel. Amongst the living pianists, Alfred Brendel is outstanding.

Autographed page of Beethoven's Moonlight *Sonata.*

Baroquelle

Beauty and Baroque

20th century loved the Baroque Age (1600-1750) that spread across France, Italy, Germany and England for its interplay of light and shade and glorious sonic brilliance.

Lets start with Italy. You can't miss Tomaso Albinoni. His delightful oboe concertos and that great adagio for the organ and strings are some of the choicest gems of the Baroque Age. But the towering giant of early Italian Baroque is Arcangelo Corelli—violinist, teacher, composer, who was Bach's senior by more than 30 years. Bach admired him greatly and even went to the extent of borrowing his themes without permission.

Corelli achieved fame almost exclusively from instrumental compositions, a very rare occurrence for that age, and built his reputation due to a boom in music publishing. Almost 80 per cent of the themes circulating in the Baroque Age were Corelli's. Theme-borrowing was a common trend of the Baroque Age and everyone borrowed tunes from everyone else. It was not considered plagiarism but an honour.

From Italy also came the famous father-son duo, Alessandro Scarlatti and Dominico. The older Scarlatti wrote beautifully for the voice—his *Stabat Mater* is a glorious work, while son Domenico was a keyboard virtuoso and his compressed and enigmatic sonatas are treasured by all great pianists.

From France came Jean-Baptiste Lully who rubbed shoulders with the great Louis XIV, whose chief musician he was. Lully formed a close musical partnership with the dramatist Molière whom Lully cheated to make a lot of money. Lully was an unpleasant sort of chap, a bit like Wagner, but an important composer. He formed an orchestra called 'Petite Bande', and was the world's first and only conductor to be killed by a baton. In those days they used to conduct by stamping the ground with a large stick and Lully's baton pierced his foot and killed him.[1]

[1] See Conducting: The Electricity In Music, Chapter 4, p. 208.

More worthy musically was the Couperin family, which was almost as prolific as the Bachs. Francois the Grand was the most important member. He was much admired by Bach and they wrote letters to each other. Couperin perfected a form of music known as 'tombeau' or memorial pieces. Written for the harpsichord they evoke memories of friends and contemporaries already in the grave. These memorial pieces were resurrected almost 400 years later by the 20th-century composer Ravel in his *Le tombeau de Couperin* in which Ravel paid homage to friends killed in World War I. In France, the late Baroque Age also produced Rameau, a composer of incomparable grace and elegance, and almost an exact contemporary of Bach. There was also Marc-Antoine Charpentier whose music is delicate and wonderfully evocative. He is enjoying a grand revival now.

In Germany, Johann Pachelbel and Georg Philipp Telemann dominated, though today Pachelbel has become a one-composition-man for his 'Canon', now a Baroque signature tune. Telemann continues to surprise being the most prolific of all the Baroque composers.

In England, Purcell remains a lone star and has survived all the vagaries of fashion. He is delicate, sensitive and lyrical. Thousands of children in this century have been introduced to classical music through a Purcell melody which made the composer Benjamin Britten create the famous *Young Person's Guide to the Orchestra*.

Like Lully did with Molière, Purcell struck a musical partnership with the poet Dryden which produced that delightful opera *King Arthur* and much more. Students of Shakespeare should not miss hearing Purcell's opera, *The Fairy Queen,* a hilarious comedy built around Puck, Bottom and the gang.

In the Baroque era, composers borrowed from each other and thought nothing about pinching a tune or two. They were not hauled to courts. Bach in his cantatas even borrowed from himself, taking a theme from an earlier work and putting it into a latter one. It is very confusing for record collectors, but at that time the composers were pretty certain that no one would make this out, as a work was not performed more than once or twice in a composer's lifetime and composers were pretty certain the audience would not remember. In the present era, with recordings permitting repeated hearings, the context of listening has completely changed.

In the last fifty years, Baroque music has gained tremendous popularity. It is music that is spectacular and strangely romantic for it was often based on other arts like literature and painting.

THE GREAT BAROQUE TREE

metaphor of the tree, when used to describe a human being, suggests solitariness as well as solidity, pioneering roots as well as inherent neglect. All this symbolically describes that great Baroque pioneer, Arcangelo Corelli (1653-1713), from whom, in a way, the entire Baroque Age in music springs to life. Corelli is sometimes called The Great Roman because in his maturity he settled down in Rome and was patronized by the clergy, including the great art collector Cardinal Ottoboni. Corelli himself was a connoisseur of art and a collector of renown. He supported contemporary painters and sculptors and after his death bequeathed his collection to Ottoboni. He specialized in Raphael who was, of course, dead by the time Corelli began collecting. The great composer expressed a desire to be buried next to Raphael and the wish was granted.

The month of December is forever associated with Corelli for his most famous work is the concerto grossi, known as the Christmas Concerto. Corelli who invented the concerto grosso form was in severe danger of being labelled a one-work composer. Fortunately, after World War II and the decades that followed, interest in Baroque music increased and research has brought to light a number of other Corelli masterpieces. He was an absolute master of the instrumental form, particularly the concerto and the sonata. There are no operas. At least, none have been discovered yet by enthusiastic music researchers.

There is no doubt that the most important Baroque form, the concerto, was discovered by Corelli. The discovery of the symphony, of course, belongs to Giovanni Battista Sammartini. It is now well proven that without Corelli's concerto grossi series we would not have had the Handel set which is much better known and which is based on the senior composer whom Handel met as a young man travelling in Italy. The two sets are so similar that, listening to both side by side, it is very difficult to make out which is Handel's and which one Corelli's. This was however no plagiarism on Handel's part. The string concerto grosso in the

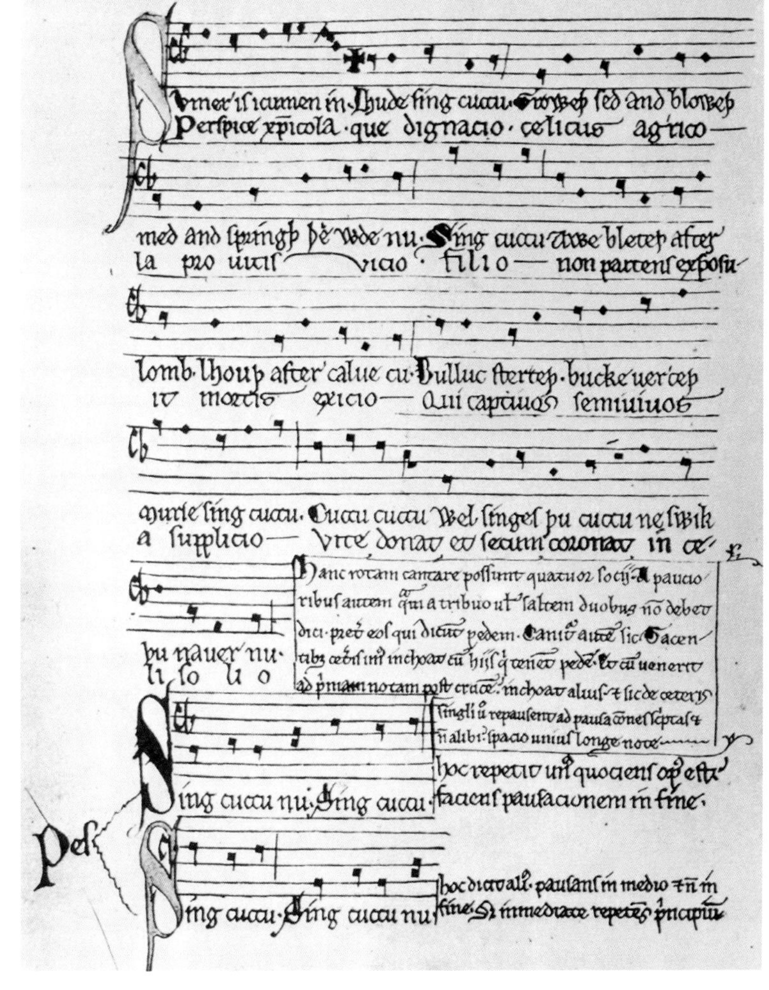

An early decorative musical manuscript. It is the song 'Summer is icumen in'.

Baroque Era has a special sound world that establishes its identity.

Corelli was an old man when he met Handel. In fact, he had heard about the famous musical contest between Dominico Scarlatti and Handel. Even if he hadn't, his friend Alessandro Scarlatti, a relation of Dominico's, would have told him about it. So, one day, when Corelli was asked to perform before Handel, the wonderful violinist was understandably nervous. The occasion has been recorded by the travelling historian Sir John Hawkins. Handel was not impressed and Corelli played out of tune. Handel, no doubt projected through the media hype of those days, had completely shattered the confidence of Corelli. Yet Corelli played the violin according to the reports written out in a diary by a pupil, George Muffat, with a brilliance reminiscent of Paganini, who was not to burst on the musical scene till the mid-19th century.

Muffat reports, 'I never met a man that suffered his passions while he was playing the violin. His eyes will sometimes turn as red as fire, his countenance will be distorted, his eyeballs roll as in agony. When he plays he doth not look the same man.' (It may interest readers to know that one of George's older relative was Thomas Muffat, whose stepdaughter Patience was the Little Miss Muffet of the well-known nursery rhyme.) Why Corelli was nervous about playing in front of Handel becomes clear if we think of the adulation that Handel received while in Italy. Corelli was then at the height of his career and Handel was just starting one.

The psychology of the creative soul is difficult to place within a frame of certainty. Corelli's rise to fame as a composer of sonatas and concertos did not happen in a smooth manner. He was refused admission to the French Academy by the composer Luigi Cherubini (1760-1842), then all-powerful in Paris. This was made more agonizing by the machinations of the court composer, Jean Baptise Lully, who drove Corelli out of Paris. Lully was also an enemy of Charpentier and made his life miserable in the Sun King's court. Lully was probably scared that both Corelli and Charpentier would draw the attention of the Sun King (Louis XIV) for, shrewd as he was, Lully must have realized that the two were the immensely superior talents.

But in his old age, Corelli received warm patronage from not only Cardinal Ottoboni but also Queen Christina of Sweden, a remarkably sensitive woman. Born into the Swedish royal family as a daughter when all were expecting a son, Christina grew up to be one of the most knowledgeable and philosophical of the European monarchs. Pity that Corelli did not keep any diaries. It would have been wonderful to read what he thought of Christina.

Corelli was very famous during his lifetime and, like a tree trunk, allowed the world of Baroque music to expand and grow with him as the centre. But soon he was forgotten. The fact that he only worked with instrumental music may have had something to do with this. Opera was then a new form and all the composers were composing operas. From Corelli's pen there are no cantatas, no oratorios, and of course, no opera. Yet with just a few works, he built a reputation for perfection that very few composers of that era can match. Corelli was like Chopin and Paganini, working within the limits of a few forms. Yet the great Roman was a composer of the first rank, an aesthetic personality without equal in music, and without whom much of the music we know and love today would not have been created.

Praying for Humanity

all the great composers, the life of Johann Sebastian Bach (1685-1750) is, apparently, the least dramatic. All the drama took place inside his mind and was reflected in his music. Bach spent most of his creative years in three small cities of 17th-century Germany and, unlike his contemporary Handel, never travelled outside the country. He lost both his parents as a child. This drew him close to his many children and to his books, music and God. As a 10-year-old, he read music by moonlight in his brother's house because he was forbidden to study scores. He walked 250 miles to listen to Buxtehude play the organ, an incident which has been recorded on a plaque in the Church of the Virgin Mary in Lubeck. He spent a month in jail in Weimar because he wanted to take up an appointment in Kothen, but the Duke of Weimar would not let him go.

Once, he fought a duel on the streets with a student as he had played the bassoon badly. The rest of Bach's life was spent in reading, learning about musical instruments and turning this knowledge into profound music. His was a life spent in devotion to God, music and his family. Bach discovered the world in music. And the world for him comprised the three small cities where he lived, married, bred children, loved God and found the meaning of God in music, as in the texts he transformed into cantatas:

> *God's time is the best of all times.*
> *In Him we live and move and*
> *have our being as He wills.*
> *In Him we die in the hour that He ordains.*

This text could be called the guiding philosophy of Bach's life—his total devotion to Lutheranism. Indeed, Bach has often been compared to Martin Luther who was also very musical and composed choral music.

Bach reading proofs of his organ music, by Batt.

The utter simplicity of Bach's life and of his music, drunk on devotion, makes him seem like a medieval saint. Nietzsche viewed Bach as being part of the Middle Ages, a sort of Saint Johann whose music feeds mankind's spiritual hunger. The *Brandenburg* Concertos, the four orchestral suites, the violin concertos, the *Well-Tempered Klavier, The Goldberg* Variations, *St. Matthew's Passion,* the Mass in B Minor, the six cello suites and, above all, the cantatas, are relevant today because, by listening to them, we emerge purified, with a sense of joy and peace in a tormented world.

Bach belonged to a musical family with a long tradition and his sons— Wilhelm Friedemann, Carl Philipp Emanuel, Johann Christoph Friedrich, and Johann Christian—used and sold a lot of his music. Even his elder brother Johann Christoph with whom Bach stayed after he had lost both his parents early in life, composed music. Bach was extremely attached to both his wives—Maria Barbara and Anna Magdalena—as they were his musical partners. He married a second time only after his first wife died under tragic circumstances. While in Kothen, Bach heard that his great contemporary Handel had come to Halle to visit his sick mother. Bach travelled on foot to meet him. Unfortunately, Handel left the city a few hours before Bach arrived. On his return, Bach heard the tragic news that his wife Maria Barbara had died. Bach married a second time primarily as he needed someone to take care of his very young sons. Anna Magdalena was his companion during the 25 years he stayed in Leipzig. Towards the end of his life, Bach wrote a few lines about Anna, which could apply equally to Maria:

You at my side, I walk with joy
To death, to my eternal rest!
O that thy gentle hands might close
My faithful eyelids in repose,
Then would my end be blessed!

Bach's wishes were fulfilled. His beloved wife was near him at the hour of his final struggle.

Johann Sebastian and his sons were not the only musical Bachs. 'If there ever was a family in which aptitude for one and the same art seemed hereditary, it must have been the Bach family,' wrote Johann Nikolaus Forkel in 1802. (Read also *The Bach Family* by Karl Geiringer) Through six generations there were scarcely two or three members of the family who did not have the gift of music. Carl Philipp was highly rated by Mozart and Haydn, and Johann Christian influenced the young Mozart. But the greatest was, of course, Johann Sebastian. I would strongly recommend the violin concertos and the *Brandenburg* Concertos, the six cello suites and the cantatas. Bach's cantatas are among the most dramatic music one could imagine. Bach composed these throughout his life, for religious and social occasions and in no other music are instruments such as the flute and the oboe used so plaintively.

There is also tremendous variety in voices—sopranos, tenors, bass and the contralto. The choral numbers are stunning and some of the orchestral introductions are quite stupendous, because of their use of trumpets and drums. One of the most amusing is the introduction to the *Peasant* Cantata, which must have given Mozart the idea for his *Musical Joke Divertimento*. Listen to the cantata for bass, *Ich Habe Genug* (I want nothing more):

I ask for nothing more
I have taken my Saviour, the hope of the pious
Into the embrace of my yearning arms.
I ask for nothing more
I have set eyes on Him.

Bach's cantatas are now being discovered throughout the musical world. In them, Bach combined the bouncy rhythm of his orchestral music with the spiritual ecstasy of his vocal music, whose results are the famous passions, leading to the point of catharsis.

The three cities where Bach lived are like the three streams of his music. In Weimer, he composed mostly organ music. Here, as a maker and repairer of organs, he raised the status of the artisan to an extraordinary level. He could also repair and build other musical instruments like the violin and the cello. The Kothen years saw the creation of some of his great instrumental music like the *Brandenburg* Concertos and the violin concertos. His last 25 years in Leipzig were spent in composing religious music like the passions[1] and the Mass. He also wrote some forms of music again and again throughout his life, like the cantatas along with the partitas for the violin and for the keyboard, organ music and the klavier books. Towards the end of his life, Bach lost his eyesight, a fact that links him with his great contemporary Handel, born in the same year. God, music and his family were his entire world, but music was like the door which led to the discovery of God in his life.

[1] Passions are basically the New Testament stories told musically.

Handel—With Love

'Baroque' meaning a misshapen or exotic pearl, really applies to Handel. His life began on an exotic note. His father, who was 60 when Handel was born, hated music. So we have the apocryphal story immortalized in paintings, of the child Handel smuggling a harpsichord into the attic and being discovered by the elders at night playing it. The child grew up to create music as flamboyant as a Rubens painting.

Was George Frideric Handel German or English? The question hasn't been settled as yet. The Germans insist Handel was German (they call him Georg Friedrich) since he was born in Halle (in 1685, the same year as Bach), and continue to perform the *Messiah* in German. The English retort by performing Handel's *Zadok the Priest* at every coronation—a convention since the anthem was first performed at the coronation of George II at Westminster Abbey where Handel was buried after his death in 1759. And, of course, they perform the *Messiah* in English and stand up whenever the 'Hallelujah' chorus is sung.

Although born a German, Handel lived for 47 years in London and became a British subject. He took his friend and lifelong companion Johann Christoph Schmidt from Germany to England and changed his name to John Christopher Smith to make it sound English. Handel was a universal musical spirit.

Handel was at heart an Italian and loved opera. Indeed the Italians can easily claim Handel as their own since the composer had Italian musical conventions at his fingertips and composed 47 Italian operas, which is the greatest Handel *terra incognita,* since these operas are even now hardly ever performed. There are good reasons for the neglect. Most of the operas are too long. Handel's *Julius Caesar* takes five hours! Imagine how long it would take on the stage! Italian opera for Handel has been like a bushel hiding his genius. A more irrational and eccentric form of entertainment can't be imagined. Handel went bankrupt several times putting up these operas—so much so that his contemporaries circulated this rhyme about Handel and his rival:

Some say compared to Bononcini,
That Mynheer Handel's but a ninny;
Others aver, that he to Handel
Is scarcely fit to hold a Candle:
Strange all this difference should be,
'Twixt Tweedle-dum and Tweedle-dee!

Today, Giovanni Bononcini (1670-1747), the court composer of Vienna, lives in music history books and Handel in the hearts of millions, not because of his operas but because of his other music like *Messiah, The Water Music* and the *Fireworks Music,* the concertos for strings and organ, and the wonderful chamber music.

Thank goodness Handel wrote the *Messiah,* which is the kind of music that transcends all barriers. Although it is traditionally music for the Christmas season, you can hear the oratorio throughout the year. Of Handel, Beethoven said, 'He is the greatest of us all.' If you meet a man who doesn't like the *Messiah,* you can do a Shakespeare on him and tell him that he 'is fit for treasons, stratagems, and spoils'!

Composers go in pairs, and the names of Handel and Bach are always linked. Yet the two Baroque masters hardly had anything in common, save that they were born in the same year, and at the end of their lives, had to have their eyes operated upon by the same surgeon, unsuccessfully. Handel was a bachelor, while Bach married twice and had 20 children! But in the land of music's immortals, the two sit hand in hand, the power and the glory of music!

Today because of the rise of good counter tenors and conductors who have specialized in the Baroque, Handel is better known. His oratorios other than the *Messiah,* like *Israel in Egypt, Susana, Theodora, Judas Maccabacus* are being recorded and performed. The songs from the operas are being sung more widely and the chamber music is being explored. The wonderful keyboard music is being recorded and some record labels like Harmonia Mundi are specialising in Handel.Windows are being opened into a fascinating world that was once confined to only a few works.

The blind Handel waits for his amanuensis, by Batt.

Orpheus Revived

Henry

Purcell is an example of how a major composer was forced to take up minor status because of neglect in his own country. Known as the 'British Orpheus' in his lifetime, Purcell was almost forgotten by the English after Handel arrived on the scene. Throughout the 18th and 19th centuries and until about 40 years ago, Purcell was put in limbo because of what is best described by an old Bengali household proverb—'The local village hermit does not get any alms.'

To give just one example, in the letters of John Keats, there are many references to Handel, but no mention of Purcell. The 19th-century English intellectuals had forgotten Purcell, arguably their greatest composer. The so-called foreign composer, Handel, had driven him out of public memory. Yet when he died in November 1695, Purcell was given the singular honour of being buried in Westminster Abbey. A newspaper report published in *The Flying Post* (23-26 November, 1695) had this to say: 'Mr. Henry Purcell, one of the most celebrated Masters of the Science of Musick in the kingdom and scarce inferior to any in Europe, dying on Thursday last; the Dean of Westminster knowing the great worth of the deceased, forthwith summoned a Chapter, and unanimously resolved that he shall be interred in the Abbey.'

Purcell was 26-years-old when Bach and Handel, the two great Baroque masters, were born in 1685. That, year Charles II died and Purcell was busy composing music for the coronation of James II who succeeded Charles. Indeed, Purcell's output created for the pleasure of the royal family—to mark coronations, birthdays and so on—was so prolific that it cast a shadow of oblivion on his best works—chamber music, the masques and his only opera, the brief and beautiful *Dido and Aeneas.*

But this was inevitable. Purcell, like most composers of that era, had to compose in order to keep the king happy and thus survive. Yet, so beautiful is Purcell's best music that he has been compared to Mozart. Both had tragically short lives, both died at 36, both were overflowing with creative genius. Purcell wrote over 500 works, comparable with Mozart's 626; both were gifted with a prodigious variety of inspiration, unrivalled psychological insight, a power of expression equally striking in sorrow and in joy and a common aptitude for the theatre.

It was through the theatre that Purcell met the poet John Dryden, 28 years older than him. The two collaborated in many productions including *King Arthur* and *The Fairy Queen*. If Mozart had Lorenzo da Ponte as his librettist, Purcell had John Dryden. The poet's unrivalled wit gives Purcell's music an added glitter.

Like Mozart, Purcell also came from a musical family of men who understood musical instruments and repaired them. The most famed, apart from our Henry, was Daniel who finds a mention in the *Oxford Dictionary of Music* as a composer and also in Greene's *Biographical Encyclopaedia of Composers*. Purcell's revival in the post-war world has been a minor miracle. Once again, it is the recording industry that has come to his rescue. Purcell has been one of the best recorded of the Baroque giants. This happened not only because Baroque music had caught the fancy of the music world. The sound world of Henry Purcell is really different, and amongst the early Baroque composers, he stands out with his calm, gentle melancholy.

The first compositions of Purcell to attract notice were his viol fantasias and his mighty *Chaccone* in G Minor. Today, the music for viola da Gamba is enjoying a revival, partly because of a film which has been made on the teacher of Marin Marias, Saint Colombe. The viola da Gamba and the viol belong to a similar sound world and Purcell's fantasias are just as beautiful as anything in Marias or Colombe. Apart from the viol, there is some exquisite music for the counter tenor voice by Purcell. The all-pervasive melancholy that Purcell communicates gives him a special place among composers of Baroque music. Purcell's was the inner voice of the Baroque—a voice once stilled by neglect, now enjoying a glorious revival.

Two of Purcell's most fascinating works are *King Arthur* and *The Fairy Queen*. The sheer poetic beauty of both was a revelation. I would like to particularly point out the famous 'cold' song from *King Arthur* in which, through unmatched dramatic music, Purcell describes the shivering cold of a relentless winter night. In this great dramatic composition, did Purcell ironically hint at his death? A musical legend says that Purcell died in a very strange way. He had the habit of drinking at the inn till the early hours of dawn. One bitterly cold December night, he returned home and his wife did not open the door. Purcell stayed outside the whole night and caught a fatal chill which developed into pneumonia and took him away at an early age.

Viva Vivaldi

you a member of the Red-Headed League? In other words, are you fond of the music of Antonio Lucio Vivaldi, the great Venetian composer also known as the Red-Headed Priest because of his shock of red hair? If 'Yes', you must be an incurable optimist, for Vivaldi's music is some of the most happy and optimistic ever written. Ezra Pound, writing in 1938 in *Guide to Kulchur,* said he was more ethereal and even more spiritual than Bach: 'There is no doubt that Bach's spirit is in great part that of a robust material world. Vivaldi moves in his adagios in the spheres of paradise.'

Although immensely successful in his lifetime, Vivaldi (1678-1741) was soon forgotten after his death. The 18th and 19th centuries hardly knew him except perhaps scholars like Brahms who made a special study of the music of the past.

Vivaldi was rediscovered in the 20th century especially after the advent of the gramophone, particularly during the LP era. Even in 1938, that great Vivaldi enthusiast Pound lamented that 'with 309 *concerti* of Vivaldi unplayed, it is useless and idiotic to think of music.'

Amongst the unheard melodies was *The Four Seasons,* which was discovered only in 1950! Now it is the recording industry's most popular music. In the pre-World War II era, amongst the many thorns that lay in the path of the popularization of the Red-Headed Priest's music, was the problem of the manuscripts. During Vivaldi's lifetime and shortly after his death, most of these were held in the private collection of the Durazzo family who had got them from the priests. One of the last surviving members of this family from Genoa was Giuseppe Maria Durazzo, a crank who refused to part with these.

However, after much persuasion, the manuscripts were printed and Vivaldi's world began to expand. But then Vivaldians developed another disease: Vivaldi was soon in danger of being branded a one-work composer.

There is much more to Vivaldi than *The Four Seasons*. Indeed, he is one of the most prolific composers of all time, and not just of the Baroque Age. He wrote concertos for a wide variety of instruments—the violin, the violoncello, the viola d'amore—an exotic instrument that sounds like a cross between the *esraj* and the *santoor*—the trumpet, the horn, the oboe, the flute, the recorder, the bassoon, the lute, the mandolin, the guitar, and even the piccolo. Apart from the concertos of which he was a master, like Mozart later, Vivaldi wrote some wonderful chamber music. His cello sonatas are spellbinding masterpieces. Being a priest, Vivaldi also wrote a lot of delightful church music.

Vivaldi would have been amused by the popularity of his *Four Seasons*. It is one of those compositions, like Beethoven's *Moonlight* Sonata, which have become symbolic of classical music. The sonnet of the *Summer* Concerto begins with these words:

In the harsh season of the hot sun
Men and animals alike languish
while the pine burns,
The cuckoo unlocks his voice and in quick accord
Both dove and goldfinch sing also.

The music is one of the first examples of programme[1] music. All the concertos have sonnets attached to them and the music describes the pictures evoked in the words.

[1] 'Programme' in music refers to a story line. In the Romantic Age, this became the tone poem, the symphonic poem, or the dramatic poem—all referring to a programme or a story which made this form of orchestral music different from the abstract symphony.

How could Vivaldi write so much music? Where did he find the time? The Red-Headed Priest, because he showed great musical talent, was excused from his pastoral duties. His health—he was also asthmatic and had heart trouble—had also something to do with it. Moreover, he was attached to a girls' hostel where all the girls were musicians. Concerts at this hostel were one of the attractions of Venice. Vivaldi found he had a captive orchestra of string and wind-players, so he went on to compose his grand series of concertos for them—a new concerto for every concert.

Vivaldi is a man for all seasons. He is a composer who is happy as a flowering tree in spring but with the capability of lapsing suddenly into a world of shadows and mysterious sadness.

OF NOTES AND LINES

I have always found the relationship between music and painting the most puzzling. Is there any connection between impressionism, expressionism, surrealism, etc., with symphonies, concertos and the rest of the musical forms? Even when a musical work describes a picture—like Rachmaninoff's tone poem *Isle of the Dead,* based on a painting by Arnold Bocklin—the music can be enjoyed without reference to that painting, creating the impression of a scintillating orchestral, albeit gloomy, outpouring of sound.

Tomás Luis de Victoria, the composer (1548-1611), and El Greco, the painter (1541-1614), lived in Spain and probably knew each other. El Greco's paintings, which in a way inspired Cubism, and his startling use of black, have been known to art connoisseurs for generations. Victoria, on the other hand, was discovered by the post-World War II generation. Nothing of Victoria was available in the LP era. Research into early music in the 1970s helped resurrect Victoria. Conductors like Paul McCreesh presented Victoria's *Requiem* and a CD of the work came into my collection. Ever since I came to know that Victoria and El Greco were contemporaries, I would think of El Greco's masterpiece, *The Burial of the Count of Orgaz,* whenever I listened to the *Requiem*. There is no document to prove that Victoria ever saw that painting but both works commemorate a royal funeral.

Somehow a cinematic image has got linked in my mind with Beethoven's Piano Sonata, op. 31, no. 1 (in G Major). Many years ago Edwin Fischer, the well-known Beethoven interpreter, wrote in an article that whenever he heard the second movement of this sonata he would visualize a castle, totally empty, its rooms covered with cobwebs, and sofas with white cloth to suggest that they were not used. As he moved through the many rooms of this castle the music moved with him. Now this was a very cinematic image, almost surreal in its fantasy, which the composer could not have imagined. Fischer was superimposing visual values to the music and I, as a listener, many years later was totally immersed in this image. As a student of literature, Fischer's response to the G Major Sonata brought to my mind Dickens's *Great Expectations* and the image of the lonely and pathetic Mrs. Havisham deserted on her wedding night, living thereafter in a castle much like the one described in Fischer's article. This is a case where the listener reads visual images that are personal and not necessarily universal in the music. To call this a sonata influenced by pictures would be wrong. Music evokes a whirlpool of feelings that communicate different associations to different people.

Now let us take a piece of music that has definite visual connotations. Claude Debussy's *The Engulfed Cathedral* describes, in the most amazing piano passages, the image of a cathedral as reflected in the water. From the outset, this music would remind me of Claude Monet's famous *Rouen Cathedral,* painted in different times of the day. Debussy, of course, knew the Impressionists, but did not create the prelude based on a specific painting. Therefore, my response once again is personal. Others may treat this magnificent piano masterpiece as an abstract collection of sounds, with no specific visual image. Both forms of appreciation are valid.

As is well known, the slow movement in Mendelssohn's *Italian* Symphony, was inspired by a procession of monks seen in Rome. The music has an infectious forward momentum. I find it exciting to go with the composer's impression and have even done a painting linking this image with that of Buddhist monks. There are others who might respond to the symphony

Portrait of the composer Victoria.

as a lovely piece of abstract music with no visual images whatsoever. I suppose it is this contradiction that Beethoven tried to convey whcn he said that the *Pastoral* Symphony was more about the feel of nature than specific images. The genius that he was, Beethoven had hit upon the dichotomy at the centre of the relationship between music and painting. Yet the same Beethoven described the second movement of his E Minor Rasoumovsky String Quartet as an evocation of a star-studded night, a splendid visual image which I find easy to accept. There is no absolute response to music, especially great music. It is like the proverbial box-within-box, and the responses could be endless and forever evolving. For instance, when I first listened to Mozart's *Haffner* Symphony, I thought of the second movement as an abstract, elegant piece of music. Now as I listen to it, I have the image of a coach moving, and wheels turning and recall the many years that Mozart spent travelling in a coach, from which his music gained a magical momentum, a sublime dynamism. The more you get to know about composers, the better your appreciation of their music will be. The same principle applies to painters and their works.

Vivaldi too used visual images in his *The Four Seasons,* which often seems like a musical counterpart of Pieter Bruegel. But painting and music really came together with Beethoven. In the Romantic Age, this relationship became a regular adventure and we find Busoni in his massive piano concerto describing paintings, and Mussorgsky describing paintings in an actual exhibition in his well-known 'Pictures at an Exhibition'.

Many serious composers today write music for films, and many great names in the 20th century, like Erich Korngold, William Walton, Prokofiev and Shostakovich, have written for the silver screen, which could not have been done without a very vivid visual imagination.

The relationship between painting and music falls into three broad categories—compositions, where the composer is inspired by a particular painting; those in which the composer unknowingly evokes strong visual images; and those that are pure abstract sounds without any reference to visuals. But the ultimate response, of course, depends on the listener.

Mozartante

The Mozart Miracle

More has been written on Wolfgang Amadeus Mozart (1756-1791) than perhaps on any other person except Jesus Christ and Beethoven. Ultimately a miracle, Mozart continues to puzzle in life and death. What effect did continuous travel have on his creative psyche? He was actually on wheels for 3,720 days in all, which comes to 10 years, 2 months and 8 days, more than a third of his life. The remaining two-thirds, he spent coming to terms with human meanness and mundane reality. At the end of it all, he was filled with delusions, hallucinations and paranoia, dying in apparent poverty though he was earning considerable amounts of money. Why? It is a question that has not yet been satisfactorily answered even after more than two hundred years. His life and death will remain one of the world's unsolved puzzles.

But there are no two opinions about his music. One of the miracles of mankind. The only problem is that there is just too much—626 works in all. Selection is inevitable and for the newcomer, it is best to divide the works into orchestral, vocal and religious music, opera and chamber music. Just remember that in Mozart there are no opus numbers but 'K' numbers because Mozart's works were catalogued by Ludwig Ritter von Köchel.

Start with the symphonies. He wrote 41 of them and the best are from no. 25 onwards. In fact, no. 25 in G Minor has become quite popular in India because it has been used in a TV commercial (the Titan watch TV commercial almost becoming a signature tune). no. 31 *Paris* is a wonderful work, and the last six—nos. 35, 36, 38, 39, 40 and 41 are outstanding. no. 41 is the famous *Jupiter* symphony whose hauntingly beautiful slow movement is arguably one of the greatest Mozart penned.

Mozart was the king of concertos. He wrote concertos for every major instrument except the cello. From his captivating set of piano concertos, highly recommended are K 271, K 466, K 467, K 482, K 488 and K 595. Try also his Flute and Harp Concerto, Bassoon Concerto, Horn Concertos and the glorious Clarinet Concerto

In praise of eight-year-old Mozart.

To all Lovers of Sciences.

THE greateſt Prodigy that Europe, or that even Human Nature has to boaſt of, is, without Contradiction, the little German Boy WOLFGANG MOZART; a Boy, Eight Years old, who has, and indeed very juſtly, raiſed the Admiration not only of the greateſt Men, but alſo of the greateſt Muſicians in Europe. It is hard to ſay, whether his Execution upon the Harpſichord and his playing and ſinging at Sight, or his own Caprice, Fancy, and Compoſitions for all Inſtruments, are moſt aſtoniſhing. The Father of this Miracle, being obliged by Deſire of ſeveral Ladies and Gentlemen to poſtpone, for a very ſhort Time, his Departure from England, will give an Opportunity to hear this little Compoſer and his Siſter, whoſe muſical Knowledge wants not Apology. Performs every Day in the Week, from Twelve to Three o'Clock in the Great Room, at the Swan and Hoop, Cornhill. Admittance 2s. 6d. each Perſon.

The two Children will play alſo together with four Hands upon the ſame Harpſichord, and put upon it a Handkerchief, without ſeeing the Keys.

Copper engraving of Emmamuel Schikanedar the librettist of Mozart's Magic Flute.

which is one of his last works and communicates the feeling of death.

Mozart's chamber music is a complete world and for many Mozartians, his greatest creation. Outstanding are the piano and wind quintet which was Mozart's own favourite work, the two piano quartets, the flute quartets, the string quintets, the oboe quartet and the clarinet quintet. Then there are the trios—the exquisite piano trios, the clarinet trio and the Divertimento for string trio (K 563), a work so unique that it stands in the history of music in a category of its own. And don't forget the violin and piano sonatas, particularly the piano sonata K 331 with the world famous rondo *alla Turca* movement.

Some of Mozart's most unique and individual creations are his divertimentos and serenades. The late *Eine Kleine Nachtmusik* is perhaps the most famous in this category. But sample too the *Serenata Notturna,* the *Posthorn* serenade and the *Serenade for 13 wind instruments,* as also the two other great wind serenades, K 375 and K 388. Indeed, every single note of Mozart's 'entertainment' music is a gem.

The best of Mozart is in his operas. Mozart's capacity for the most captivating melodies and his dramatic instincts and sense of fun make the operas irresistible. It may not be possible to listen to all, but try *The Abduction from the Seraglio, The Marriage of Figaro, Don Giovanni,* and of course, *The Magic Flute,* which has the most heavenly music ever composed.

Mozart wrote religious music throughout his life. His *Requiem,* because of its mysterious association with a messenger of death, has become a cult composition. But listen also to the sunlit *Exsultate Jubilate* for soprano and strings with the scintillating *Hallelujah* and the brilliant *Coronation Mass.*

It is really impossible to offer an 'Eine Kleine Mozart' out of his oeuvre. What you leave out is probably as beautiful as what you recommend.

The Mozart Express Moves On

other day, thanks to a friend, a musical treasure came into my hands—the January 1956 Mozart birth centenary issue of the magazine *Music and Musicians*. The magazine reminded me of how musical times have flown as far as Mozart is concerned. After all, just a few years ago in 1991, we observed the bicentenary of Mozart's death.

How things change. *Amadeus,* the film made Mozart a household name overnight. There was Mozart confectionery, Mozart underwear, Mozart hotels, Mozart express trains, Mozart airlines...they were even thinking of naming a satellite after Mozart! Philips, who invented the CD, announced that they were going to record every single work of Mozart—every little thing that Mozart had composed, including all the incomplete fragments.

It was certainly a different story in 1956, as the magazine demonstrates. Mozart was then far from being a mania and Mozartina was a concept not even dreamt of.

The fortunes of all composers undergo a gradual evolution. But the Mozart case is probably unique. Soon after his death, people realized his greatness first spread by composers like Beethoven, Haydn, Rossini and Chopin, to mention a few. When Chopin was on his deathbed in Paris, his friends wanted to perform his works for him. But Chopin said, 'Play me some Mozart in my memory.' A major landmark for Mozart was the publication (close to his birth anniversary) of the catalogue by Ludwig Ritter von Köchel. Still, in 1956 the great Mozart scholar Harry Blech, conductor of the London Mozart Players, wrote: 'The concert-going public does not always realize that after all these years, it is not only still impossible to get reliable scores and material for some of Mozart's works, but that quite a number have in fact never been printed,'—quite a far cry from the situation today when we have all of Mozart on authentic period instruments, as well as the romanticized Mozart. The composer got another boost in 1891 when his death anniversary was observed with

DIE ZAUBERFLÖTE

eine

GROSSE OPER IN ZWEY AUFZUGEN

fürs

CLAVIER oder PIANOFORTE

von

W. A. MOZART.

Illustration showing the bird-catcher Papageno in a piano arrangement of Mozart's Magic Flute.

George Bernard Shaw, then a leading music critic, playing a major role with articles and concerts. But even so, the popularity graph rose slowly.

Take the case of his portraits. The famous painting, unfinished, of Mozart by his brother-in-law Joseph Lange, which is on the cover of the bicentenary issue of the magazine, is today found on chocolate tins. But forty years ago it was hardly known and the magazine took a lot of trouble to explain the origin of the painting. In the same issue, the great Neville Cardus wrote a brilliant essay comparing for the first time Mozart's *The Magic Flute* and Shakespeare's *The Tempest,* where he says, 'I have never read or heard that any commentator on *The Magic Flute* has pointed out, or even forced, a resemblance between the Sarastro-Pamina-Tamino story and the Prospero-Miranda-Ferdinand of *The Tempest.*' Today, every critic talks about this parallel.

In a remarkable essay on the Mozart piano concertos, the famous critic William Mann writes about the world-famous C Major Concerto (K 467), now known as *Elvira Madigan* because it was the background score of that film. Forty years ago, its charms had to be advocated and Mann wrote about the slow movements of the entire group: 'In the slow movements, the chief thing one notices is that most of them are andantes rather than adagios, that is gently-flowing, nocturnal music more than slow, tragic or deeply emotional pieces. One reverie is the andante of the C Major Concerto, K 467, which is based on a long, celestially-flowing tune that hovers above a plucked string accompaniment—the only word fitting for such music is "dreamy".' It is a quaint description of what is one of classical music's most famous and frequently recorded moments. Today, Mozart's piano concertos are often recorded by the pianist playing and conducting from the keyboard. It has become standard practice with the vogue for original instruments. But at the time when Mann wrote his path-breaking article, it was not so. He pointed this out: 'Today, the situation has changed dramatically and it is the exception to use a conductor in a Mozart piano concerto.'

A revealing article is the 'Mozart on Disc' by David Hunt: 'Proof, if proof were needed that Mozart's music is at least coming to be appreciated at its true worth, is afforded by the fact that since the invention of the gramophone, more Mozart has been recorded than the music of any other single composer.' He writes in his article about the performances on record, which in today's CD era, have become legendary performances and are being reissued, like the horn concertos by the great Dennis Brain, one of the greatest of all horn virtuosos who died tragically young in a car accident, and the serenades and divertimentos by the conductor Peter Maag. But Hunt complains that the piano concertos are still not well represented. He talks about a jubilee edition from Philips which eventually resulted in all the works being put on LP.

Mozart is truly a joy forever and each centenary will be a landmark. Just as today, a 1956 magazine on Mozart seems quaintly nostalgic, the coming century will find the Mozart mania of the present equally strange. This century will perhaps find a new way to appreciate this most divinely gifted of composers.

A Great Musical Friendship

I would like to recall a wonderful and noble human relationship that enriched the life of Mozart, the like of which had not happened in the music world before or since. Mozart was the son of Leopold, the court violinist and composer of Salzburg. But he was destined to become the adopted son of another man, also a composer, who was 24-years-old in 1756. His name was Joseph Haydn. Mozart, as we all know, was a child prodigy. His name soon spread far and wide and he became a celebrity at the age of five. But Haydn was a slow starter. When Mozart was born, Haydn had hardly composed anything —an organ concerto and a piano concerto. That was all. He was soon about to hear of the extraordinary genius Mozart, but they were not destined to meet till 1781.

By that eventful year, both composers were famous. Haydn had established the string quartet and the symphony, and Mozart had composed prolifically, including the opera *Idomeneo,* the *Paris* Symphony, and violin and piano concertos. When they met, Haydn was 49-years-old and Mozart was 25.

They took to each other instantly and began to meet regularly in Vienna to play string quartets together. Mozart, otherwise cantankerous and suspicious by nature, took to Haydn like a duck to water. And Haydn, who was childless, started feeling fatherly towards the younger composer.

Mozart, when he met Haydn, was in need of emotional stability. He was looking for a father figure and a guide. He had been kicked out of Salzburg and was living in Vienna as a freelancer. He was developing a cold war with his father who did not approve of Mozart's decision to marry. His meeting with the man whom everybody called 'Papa' was very fortuitous.

After the initial meeting, whenever Haydn came down to Vienna from the Hungarian estate Esterhazy where he was the court composer, Mozart would invite him to his house.

Their mutual regard blossomed into friendship and reached a pinnacle when Mozart dedicated six string quartets to Haydn. The quartets are known as

The dedication page of Mozart's Haydn *Quartets.*

the *Haydn* Quartets. Mozart made a written dedication to Haydn.

When we remember Mozart's remarkable talent for puns, anagrams and *double entendres*, his habit of playing with his friends by signing his letters as 'Trazom', his famous letter to Haydn cannot be read as a simple musical dedication. It is an appeal from an orphan to a prospective father figure. The dedication begins with the words, 'A father having resolved to send his sons into the great world finds it advisable to entrust them to the protection and guidance of a highly celebrated man, more so since this man by a stroke of luck is his best friend...'

It is a fact that men often find it hard to express strong feelings for each other. Intensely affectionate but emotionally unstable, Mozart was trying to express his feelings through this letter. Having been, like his music, sent into this great world, he was incapable of managing his own affairs. For such a man, what could be more desirable than the protection and guidance of a highly celebrated man? Mozart was hinting to the older man how much he needed his protection in unfriendly Vienna, not only musically but emotionally as well.

Haydn, of course, returned the compliment by declaring to the world that Mozart was the greatest composer he had known.

Unfortunately, Mozart was not destined to enjoy the friendship for long. Destiny moved at an electrifying and all-consuming tempo to pull them apart. Haydn was invited to go to London. Mozart was totally against Haydn's going to London. But Haydn was eager for a

SEI

QUARTETTI

PER DUE VIOLINI, VIOLA, E VIOLONCELLO

Composti e Dedicati

al Signor

GIUSEPPE HAYDN

Maestro di Cappella di S.A.

il Principe d'Esterhazy &c &c

Dal Suo Amico

W.A.MOZART

Opera X.

In Vienna presso Artaria Comp

Mercanti ed Editori di Stampe Musica.

e Carte Geografiche

change of scene and for him London meant a change from the binding routine of court life. Mozart had been to London as a child prodigy. There he had met Bach's son Johann Christian, known as the 'London Bach.' He had travelled to most of the great cities of the world. Haydn, at sixty, had hardly seen anything beyond the marshes that surrounded the castle of Esterhazy where he lived. Mozart was genuinely worried about his friend who was basically a simple peasant and who knew no English. Would Haydn succeed in sophisticated London? Perhaps Mozart felt sorry that the only man for whom he felt genuine love in a hostile world was being snatched away.

The day of departure came—15 December, 1790. Haydn spent the last day with Mozart. Both were strangely shaken by the parting and wept bitterly. Mozart, desperately anxious for his friend's safety and for his own future in a friendless world, cried out bitterly, 'I fear, Father, this will be our last farewell.' These were prophetic words and this was a strange parting, for within a year, Mozart was dead.

Although he bade farewell to Haydn, his own health was the last thing on his mind and he was, in fact, planning a trip to London. Mozart was actually more worried about his older friend. He felt that Haydn would be cheated in the musical rat race of London. But, as it turned out, Haydn managed quite well. Not only did he compose his greatest symphonies through the London interaction but he also studied the English Oratorio and returned to Germany to compose the masterpieces of his old age: *The Creation and The Seasons*.

But no such luck awaited his young friend Mozart.

Haydn heard of Mozart's death in London. He was quite inconsolable and paid him a musician's tribute by composing and dedicating the slow movement of a new symphony, no. 98 in B flat, based on a free variation on the anthem *God Save the King*, to Mozart. This was a personal tribute that only Haydn could have paid. In words he said, 'The world will not see a talent like Mozart in hundreds of years.' Truly, here was a friendship which, like their music, comes but rarely to remind us that friendship and love exist no matter what the cynics say.

Haydn and Skullduggery

of the most bizarre music stories I have ever read was on that most loveable of all composers, Joseph Haydn. Haydn was probably one composer who never had an enemy in his life. He earned the friendship of Mozart, who was 25 years his junior and who called him 'Papa'. Later on, this word 'Papa' got linked with Haydn, though the history of the symphony through modern research has proved that Haydn was not the father of the symphony. That credit should go to Giovanni Battista Sammartini and the Italian school of composers.

In his old age, Haydn earned the respect of the young Beethoven in Vienna, though he was shocked by some of the innovations in Beethoven's early music. He was the least controversial of all the great composers, respectful towards authority, and the perfect court composer—the court in Haydn's case being the Hungarian princely family of Esterhazy from whom he enjoyed lifetime patronage. Yet why was Haydn, who began all his compositions with the words *'In Nomine Domini'* (in the name of God), not left in peace after his death?

The story about the disappearance of Haydn's skull after he was buried reminds me of the famous anecdote concerning his canons. In his bedroom, Haydn had hung a set of 24 canons that he had composed. 'I am not rich enough,' said Haydn, 'to buy paintings, so I have found myself hangings that few others would possess.' When his wife complained one day that there was not enough money in the house to bury him if he were to die, Haydn replied, 'If such a calamity occurs, take the canons out of the frame and sell them to a publisher. I am sure they will cover a decent funeral.' He did not know then that he would have not one but three burials.

The strange story is told by the husband and wife team of musicologists, Miriam and Kurt Blaukopf from Vienna: 'It has taken a long time for Joseph Haydn to find peace since he was placed in his grave in 1809.' (This burial of the 77-year-old composer in a Vienna

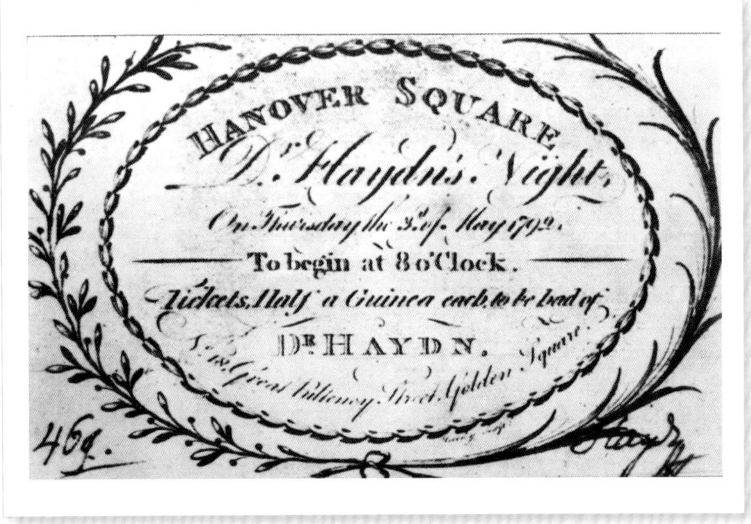

Publicity for a Haydn's concert.

ravaged by war is poignantly told by Haydn's biographer Rosemary Hughes in *Master Musicians* biography published in 1950 though the writer is silent about the skull incident.) 'It is now history,' continues the Blaukopf duo, 'that a few days after his burial, a group of eager phrenologists, anxious to prove their theories, stole the skull in the dead of night from the newly made grave. At that time in Vienna and in a great deal of Europe, the theories propounded by the famous Viennese phrenologist Franz Joseph Gall were in circulation. Gall suggested that particular traits of the mind and character were denoted by the specific bone structure of the human skull.' Being a famous musician, Haydn was worth studying by what is commonly known as 'reading the bumps'. This was the first burial. Naturally, the theft was not discovered.

Meanwhile, Haydn's patrons, the Esterhazy family, planned a grand mausoleum in his honour. Eleven years later, the mausoleum in the Esterhazy family chapel in Eisenstadt was completed. Then the prince ordered the exhumation of Haydn's body for reinternment in the new splendid resting place. 'But when the grave was opened on 30 October 1820, to everyone's horror, the body was seen to be without a head. What remained was transferred to the mausoleum and immediately the prince instituted a house-to-house search for the missing skull.' Judging by what happened to Haydn after the burial, perhaps it would have been better if he too had been buried in a pauper's unknown grave like his beloved Mozart.

To continue the history of Haydn's skull after the 1820 discovery—a hunt was carried out which reads like a Sherlock Holmes search. The skull was eventually found to be in the possession of the celebrated anatomist Rokitansky, whose family decided to give it to the Society of the Friends of Music in Vienna. The Society placed it in a glass case in their library where it remained for 145 years.

In 1932, Haydn's bicentenary, it was decided that the skull should be returned to Haydn's body in the mausoleum at Eisenstadt. The Rokitansky family, however, had stipulated in their will that the skull could not leave the Society of the Friends of Music. But the lawyers consulted the fine print and a legal battle ensued, and for more than 45 years, the Vienna City Council

Haydn at Esterhazy, by Batt. This was Haydn's summer house, a gift from the Esterhazy family.

and the music lovers of Vienna had the vision of making a pilgrimage to the grave with the skull in hand. But they had to wait until 5 June 1954, when the skull was finally reunited with the body of the famous composer.

At a solemn ceremony where Mozart's *Requiem* and Haydn's beautiful *Nelson Mass* were played, Haydn's body was exhumed for the third time and the skull was put back in place, in the presence of the modern Count Esterhazy. To the sound of the *Mass* and the *Requiem,* the heavy lid, weighing nearly half-a-ton, decorated with white marble Baroque angels, was swung into place and finally closed.

I was both fascinated and surprised by this story because I have been, over the last 40 years, very

Facing page: Haydn's musical visiting card with its own melody. Below: Score from Haydn's Creation.

intimate with the music of this great Austrian composer. In the various books and articles I have read about Haydn, I have not located a sequel to this skull tale. It was a kind of skullduggery, though done in the name of science. One assumes that 50 years on, Haydn rests in peace in the castle where he composed most of his symphonies, concertos, string quartets, piano sonatas, oratorios, operas and Masses, and those wanting a friendship with one of the warmest and most refreshingly happy composers will do themselves no harm in saying hello to the 'Papa' of classical music.

Romantica

The Last of the Caesars

There is something imposing about the name Brahms (1833-1897). Pronounce it and the syllables sound like the closing bars of a symphony. Brahms, in fact, can be considered the end of the classical sound in music. He has been called the last of the Caesars. An anachronism. A classicist in the Romantic Age.

Brahms is like caviar, an acquired taste. Many find him heavy, over-serious, even obscure. For the great Neville Cardus, Brahms was the ideal desert island composer. Cardus felt that Brahms offers the best of every form except opera. And on a desert island, the chances of an opera production are remote. Cardus once made a list of what he would take with him on exile. Brahms' four symphonies, each so different from the other—the first intensely tragic, with a great theme at the end reminiscent of Beethoven's *Choral* Symphony, a fact that has made some people term it the Tenth after Beethoven's Ninth. Brahms, of course, said, 'Any fool can see the resemblance, but it is what I have done to it that matters.' The second symphony is absolutely

Brahms makes his morning cup of coffee, by Batt.

Right: Johannes Brahms as a young man.
Below right: Johann Strauss and Brahms in the garden in Strauss' home.

ravishing—a pastoral, lyrical music that sounds like paradise. The third is epigrammatic, and a terse statement of intense beauty. The fourth has the most unusual beginning in all symphonic literature, as if Brahms was plucking a theme from the sky. It is the symphony that the majority of Brahmsians love most.

Brahms was a master of the variation form, and Cardus selected the wonderful *Haydn* Variations and the *Handel and Paganini* Variations. According to him, Brahms has said the last word on this very difficult form. When it comes to the concerto, Brahms offers the best in violin and piano; two of the most important instruments in the concerto form. His two piano concertos are simply staggering.

The first is romantic and was written after he had fallen in love with Clara Schumann, a woman fourteen years older than him. It was love beyond longing, and all the pain and turmoil is in his work. The second concerto was written when Brahms was an old man, recollecting passion in tranquility. If music can be a philosophical document, this concerto is it. The slow movement of this concerto has a theme for the cello which is like frozen tears. Brahms also wrote a double concerto for the violin and cello, which is a favourite with all great instrumentalists. The beautiful violin concerto, the mightiest after Beethoven, completes the Brahmsian essay in the concerto form.

In choral music, Brahms produced an incredible masterpiece in the *German Requiem,* written after his mother's death. It is called a *German Requiem* because it uses German poems on life and death, instead of the usual Latin text.

Brahms at the piano.

Listen to this profound music, particularly the baritone song about the end of life.

Brahms, like Beethoven, was not a prolific composer. He destroyed much and published only what he and Clara Schumann passed. Clara was his editor, and he valued her judgement. But he did write a great deal of chamber music, and it is this group that, according to Cardus, tilts the scale towards Brahms when it comes to choosing the ideal desert island composer.

In his chamber music, it is difficult to give a recommendation. All of it is worth listening to. But the most unusual are the piano quintet, the three piano quartets, the two glorious string sextets which greats like Pablo Casals and Yehudi Menuhin were so fond of playing, and the striking group of works Brahms wrote for the clarinet in his last years. They contain music for meditation tinged with pathos, and a nostalgic twilight mood. Also try the two string quintets, the piano trios and the romantic trio for horn, violin and piano. This last work has perhaps the most unusual theme ever written for horn, with a melody like a long meandering train.

What makes Brahms sound so special? Perhaps it is the sound of sadness. Perhaps, Brahms strikes in all of us that twinge of sorrow, and by bringing it into focus, achieves a catharsis. Brahms achieved this quality because throughout his life he, as the poet Shelley would put it, felt: 'The desire of the moth for the star, the night for the morrow.' Clara Schumann remained a lifetime friend. They never married. She died a year before him, and he followed her to the grave soon afterwards. It was all over at sixty-four.

Towards the end of his life, Brahms wrote some wonderful compositions tinged with a pensive nostalgia that for many Brahmsians are the eternal companions of old age. They are the clarinet quintet, and the incomparable *Alto* Rhapsody. This work for a contralto and orchestra was written at the height of his maturity, after he had fallen in love with Schumann's daughter, Julie, and had discovered her marrying someone else. Brahms also wrote beautifully for the piano, including some glorious violin and piano sonatas.

Whether you travel down to a desert island or stay in the city, listen to Brahms. He will become a lifelong passion.

A Little Wild, A Little Mad

Portrait of Hector Berlioz.

It is not often that the flow of music has erupted like a volcano in the middle of the sea. That's precisely what happened when that great French composer Hector Berlioz (1803-1869) burst on the scene around 1830, the year in which his world-famous *Symphonie Fantastique* was premiered. Berlioz has been described as a freak and a prophet. Throughout his stormy, uneasy life, he was labelled a genius by some and reviled by others. Possibly the most original Romantic composer, Berlioz was driven by a unique musical vision that went far beyond his time.

Of all the great composers, Berlioz probably had the most fantastic life. Like Charles Dickens' hero Pip, Berlioz had a childhood sweetheart whom he could not marry. Like in a Bollywood film, Berlioz in his old age went to search for his childhood love, found her and the old couple lived happily ever after. Love never died in Berlioz's life. He is the only composer who married a musical theme. It happened this way. Berlioz had fallen in love with a Shakespearean actress, Harriet

Liszt plays the piano. Berlioz stands enthralled.

Smithson. She refused him. In his frustration, Berlioz created the immortal *Symphonie Fantastique* in which Harriet becomes a *femme fatale* in the form of a fixed musical theme. (This was a Berlioz innovation which Wagner borrowed years later and called it a leitmotif.) Anyway, after the symphony was premiered, Harriet relented and married Berlioz only to find that musical themes and marriage made strange bedfellows. They were soon divorced. Berlioz married a second time and eventually lost both his wives to return to his original sweetheart à la Bollywood.

Berlioz was a master of innovations, both in life and music. His entry into music was dramatic. He had been sent to study medicine, but the sight of blood in the dissection theatre made the sensitive Berlioz jump out of the window. He never returned and soon turned to composing. Two facts make Berlioz a historically important and crucially valuable composer. No other composer—not even Mendelssohn and Verdi—understood the essence of Shakespeare better than Berlioz. His Shakespearean empathy was strong because he was himself a brilliant writer. His memoirs remain a classic of the Romantic Age, and can be read not just for musical information, but also as a great piece of literature. His *King Lear* overture and the symphony *Romeo and Juliet* were path-breaking pieces which forged a relationship between literature and music and paved the way for the world of Richard Wagner, Tchaikovsky, Gustav Mahler, Richard Strauss and Sergei Prokofiev.

Berlioz was also the music world's most brilliant orchestrator. Not only did he write a book on

Gustave Dore's etching of satan. Satanic problems have been a concern of the romantic composers like Liszt and Berlioz.

orchestration which has become a standard text book, but also actually experimented with the blending of the human voice and instruments, which immensely helped composers like Wagner, Mahler and Richard Strauss in future. His *Damnation of Faust, Romeo and Juliet, Requiem* and the extraordinary *Symphonie Funèbre et Triomphale* are great monuments of orchestral writing whose originality makes one understand why the poet Heine called Berlioz an 'immense nightingale' and 'a lark as great as an eagle'.

Surprisingly, the greatest modern exponent of this French composer is an Englishman, Sir Colin Davis, and his unique recordings of all the operas, overtures and symphonies have made Berlioz more popular today than he has ever been. Indeed, the Berlioz mystique is most beautifully expressed in the work *Harold in Italy,* a disguised viola concerto which Berlioz composed for Paganini. The great violinist refused to play the work because he thought the viola part was not brilliant enough. Today it is considered the greatest musical monument to this much neglected musical instrument which was incidentally Mozart's favourite fiddle.

In the hands of Berlioz, the orchestra became a rustling forest where singing birds called to one another, where the roars of the lion were heard in the distance and thunderstorms broke out suddenly. His magic can be best understood by studying the paintings of Delacroix, a great friend of Berlioz. Like the painter, Berlioz's music is a study in brilliant and tempestuous contrasts.

A Web of Magic

Maria von Weber is one of the great shadowy figures of Western music. He is often overshadowed by Beethoven and Schubert, his two exact contemporaries, and the fact that he launched the Romantic Age in all its mysterious and supernatural force and glory is often forgotten. When Weber was born in 1786, Mozart's last great operas were being launched, and when he died in 1826, Beethoven and Schubert were still alive.

Weber's mother had tuberculosis, so he was not blessed with robust health. But it was music that replenished him. Weber's father, Franz Anton's interest in lithography and musical drama ensured his son an artistic education. Weber was a trained painter as well as musician, and grew up to be the complete artist of the Romantic Age. But not before father Franz put Weber through a lot of trouble, getting him arrested for treason once and, on another occasion, making him swallow nitric acid by mistake which almost certainly destroyed his already tubercular lungs. Incidentally, one of Weber's music teachers was the famous 'Abt' Vogler on whom Robert Browning wrote his great poem.

Since Weber raised the curtain on the Romantic Age, it is appropriate at this point to say a few words about what the 19th century expected from its composers. The 19th century was an age of great versatility. Thinkers, philosophers and artists looked, read and heard between the lines. The text or the score unfolded layers and layers of meaning and nuances. Thus we find composers like Weber, Berlioz, Schumann and Wagner straddling many media, using the pen, the brush and the musical note with consummate ease. Weber was a trained lithographer, the first truly modern conductor with the baton and podium manners, a sharp-witted music critic, pianist and writer.

But Weber's greatest contribution was the creation of the supernatural and mysterious world and the evocation of fantasy. Perhaps the most famous opera of the supernatural is Weber's *Der Freischutz* or 'The Marksman'. The libretto or the text is based on *The Book*

Weber conducting.

of Ghosts by Apel and Launs, and the opera represents the triumph of the German Romantic opera. The very spirit of nature comes alive in the forest scenes with the hunting horns and sounds of the chase, and the fullness of village life with its dancing and prize shooting. Especially beautiful are the woodland poetry of the happy folk, the sinister and mysterious Wolf's Glen, the picturesquely villainous Kaspar and the terrifying figure of Samiel. The overture is astounding too and a favourite in the concert hall. The casting of the magic bullets that never miss is at the heart of the opera, and its evocation in music with the howling storm and the hooting of owls, spectres and a gibbering death's head, brought forth from Weber some astonishing music that inspired Wagner later.

Weber's supernatural world does not end with *Freischutz*. At the end of his short life, Weber composed *Oberon* almost on popular demand, for the English audience. (Like Mendelssohn later, Weber was extremely popular in England. He died there too.) *Oberon* is partly based on Shakespeare's *A Midsummer Night's Dream* and partly on Christoph Martin Wieland's epic poem *Oberon*. Although suffering from advanced tuberculosis, Weber travelled to London to conduct the rehearsals of the first performance of the opera. Weber's ethereal and fancy-filled music conjured up with magic horn-calls the shimmering gossamer world of Shakespeare's play.

The ravishing world of Weber is not only confined to opera. This composer, whose cousin married Mozart and whose daughter-in-law, much later, fell in love with Mahler, wrote some enchanting instrumental music. No other composer, except perhaps Mozart, and later, Brahms, has written so excitingly for the clarinet. Weber wrote two clarinet concertos, both utterly charming. So is the clarinet quintet, which ranks as one of the three greatest clarinet quintets written; the other two being those of Mozart and Brahms.

Weber also wrote beautifully for the bassoon and the guitar, and his two piano concertos are outstanding. Listen to his violin and piano sonatas, a set of music possessing quaint charm. His piano sonatas are now becoming popular

Weber is a master composer of great individuality and beauty. He is never dull. His orchestration is absolutely astonishing. And his sound world is so special that you cannot mistake it for that of anyone else. The Romantic Age has many composers, but none as onomatopoeic as Weber.

The Essence of Innocence

Portrait of Schubert.

Of all the great composers, Franz Schubert (1797-1828) was the one who was totally Viennese. Throughout his 31 years, he hardly left that city except on short holidays. As he was completely Viennese, his music has a special feel which can best described as the apotheosis of the dance.

Schubert's music revels in the way the human mind revels after good triumphs over evil. His melodies are intoxicating such as the opening and the last movement of The *Great C Major* Symphony, the second movement of the glorious *Unfinished* Symphony, the opening of the Piano Trio in B flat whose melody inspired the popular song 'Over the Waves', much of the Trout and the Cello Quintets, and many of the movements of his stunning range of piano sonatas. This list is very short, and as you listen to Schubert's music, you'll make your own list of favourites.

An autographed manuscript of Schubert's songs.

Small, unattractive and tubby, Schubert's short life was rather uneventful. It is ironical that Mozart's greatest enemy, Salieri (who is now being discovered as a composer of considerably attractive music), was a teacher of the composer who is often described as being blessed by Mozart. Salieri, at the end cheated Schubert by recommending a rival to a court appointment, which could have brought Schubert the money he badly needed.

Schubert's unquestioning trust in human beings makes him come across as the most human of all composers. The eyes that stare through the round spectacles in his many portraits are kind, even tender and loving. Schubert loved his friends and was loved in return. Indeed, without his friends, Schubert wouldn't have survived in such a hostile world. They arranged the publication of his works, raised funds for concerts, and created the atmosphere for the once-a-week *Schubertiads,* where Schubert could premiere and present his creations. His life is like a long series of intimate conversations over coffee and wine with his friends. This gives Schubert the peculiar yet familiar charm of being the boy next door and surely sets him apart from other composers.

A brief life with brilliant music—that's Schubert. But the question is, how does one approach him musically? Schubert was so prolific that it is not possible to listen to all that he wrote. One could concentrate on key works and glean the essence.

Let us begin with the symphonies. Start with the Fifth Symphony which is like a bouquet of enchanting melodies, a combination of Mozart's last E flat Symphony and Beethoven's *Pastoral* Symphony. After this, move on to the dark-hued *Unfinished,* in two movements (hence the title). The symphony has the most unforgettable beginning on low strings, like ripples over a darkly lit sea. The melody of the second movement was described by a critic as a child stroking the head of a grief-stricken man. Finally, come to *The Great Symphony* in C Major, which is intense and fiery, like a wild primitive dance.

Schubert wrote no concertos, but a great number of chamber works and sonatas and miscellaneous instrumental works. There are also over 600 songs. Here lies the true Schubert, the most gifted melodist in the world of Western music. The quality of his works is so uniformly good that you can't go wrong with a random selection. But don't forget the two piano trios—the Trout and Cello Quintets, and the Impromptus. The piano sonatas too are ravishing, particularly the one in B flat.

Schubert's religious music is profoundly striking, with an innocence about it, like a child writing letters to God. And don't forget Schubert wrote perhaps the most famous melody in church music—*Ave Maria*—based on a poem by Walter Scott. Of all the composers, he and Dvorak are the two I would love to have met.

Schubert is often compared to Mozart. Both were spontaneous, prolific and inspired composers. But the resemblance ends there. Schubert was born six years after Mozart's death, and died one year after Beethoven. He was a pallbearer at Beethoven's funeral, and was an exact contemporary of that great composer though they hardly knew each other. Weber was another contemporary. Schubert lacked Mozart's dramatic sense—that's why his operas were a failure. That ruined him financially and had a direct effect on his mental happiness. The early years of the Romantic century was the age of the opera—the entertainment the public wanted. But it was pure song that was Schubert's genius, not drama. He sang like a bird overpowered by spring. Even his Masses, like the great E flat Mass, sings in spontaneous joy. Mozart, in his instrumental music, creates abstract patterns. Schubert suggests ideas that can be visualized concretely. He was the child of his age, the quintessential Romantic.

The Renaissance Romantic

concept of the Renaissance spirit, the versatile man of arts, returned in the Romantic Age. And no one was more dexterous than Felix Mendelssohn (1809-1847). Born into a wealthy Jewish family that encouraged his talents, Mendelssohn blossomed into a painter, writer, editor, conductor, musicologist, poet, linguist, mountaineer, pianist and composer. That German proverb, 'If I rest, I rust' applied only too well to this child prodigy who worked so relentlessly that he simply collapsed from exhaustion and died at the age of 38.

Mendelssohn's sudden death sent two nations into mourning: England and Germany. Like Weber before him, Mendelssohn charmed the English with his music and manners. He was Queen Victoria's music teacher and a personal friend of Prince Albert. After his death, the Queen wrote personally to his wife, Cecile—an unprecedented gesture from an English monarch.

Mendelssohn's death is inevitably connected with his sister Fanny with whom he had a most passionate and complex relationship, the significance of which

Mendelssohn's cartoon by Aubrey Beardsley .

Andante
Organ
Hear my prayer, O God incline thine ear! Thyself from my pe-
tition do not hide Hear my prayer O God incline thine ear thyself from my petition do not
hide, thyself from my petition do not hide thyself from my petition do not hide take heed to me
Cresc.
Cresc.
hear how in prayer I mourn to thee, hear how in prayer I mourn to thee hear how in prayer I
mourn to thee! Take heed to me Take heed to me! Without thee all is dark I have no guide

An autographed manuscript of Mendelssohn's song 'Hear my Prayer' - the Fifty-Fifth Psalm.

continues to puzzle Mendelssohn scholars. Fanny, supposed to have had 'Bach fugue fingers', according to her mother, would probably have become a famous composer had she lived in the 20th century. But she was always made to play second fiddle to Felix, who even suggested that her compositions be published in his name since society couldn't accept a female composer. In 1847, Felix was shattered when his sister died, and he never recovered from the blow. Cecile followed him six years later, utterly inconsolable, at the age of 36.

Felix and Fanny together gave the music world one of its greatest treasures which was almost lost—the music of Johann Sebastian Bach.

Every lover of Bach, particularly of his great passions and his choral music, should be eternally grateful to Mendelssohn and his sister. The two worked tirelessly in old monasteries and libraries to retrieve Bach's *St. Matthew's Passion,* which Mendelssohn conducted. Before this, Bach was considered 'a powdered wig stuffed with learning'. Said Mendelssohn, 'To think that a Jew should give to the people the greatest Christian music in the world.'

During his short lifetime, Mendelssohn fascinated Goethe with his piano-playing and his music. His compositions had their ups and downs. Wagner did him much harm because he was a Jew-hater, but more so because he was jealous. Wagner always yearned for the family background Mendelssohn had, and hardly a day passed without the former saying or writing something critical about the latter. There can be no doubt that the Romantics influenced each other from generation to generation. Weber influenced Mendelssohn, and he, in turn, influenced and obsessed Wagner. But in the 20th century, Mendelssohn's popularity pendulum swing back and forth. He was regarded as a 'song without words'—a composer of sweet nothings; a view that was most unfair. But today it's good to find his art being recognized as the logical development of Mozart through Weber.

Indeed, Mendelssohn should be approached through the symphonic form. He wrote five scintillating ones, and countless minor sinfonias. The most famous of the symphonies are no. 3 (*Scotch*) and no. 4 (the *Italian*). no. 5 (*Reformation*) is a moving work, and no. 2 (*Lobgesang* or Hymn of Praise) is a wonderful example of Mendelssohn's choral skills. This symphony will remind Wagnerites of *Parsifal.* Mendelssohn's choral works are worth sampling. He took the English choral tradition, to which he was exposed, to new heights of creative expression. His chamber music too is worth exploring, particularly the *Songs Without Words,* his marvellous octet and his cello sonatas. Sample also the string quartets, one of which is a funeral ode to Fanny.

Mendelssohn is most popular for his overtures, especially the incidental music to Shakespeare's *A Midsummer Night's Dream.* For many, though, his violin concerto and two piano concertos in G Minor and D Minor are the best. Mendelssohn may not have been as prolific as Mozart or Bach, but whatever he wrote has the stamp of perfection and simplicity.

Listener's Choice

Franz

Liszt (1811-1886) was the most stupendously theatrical of all the Romantics, running a close neck-to-neck race for flamboyance with George Gordon Byron. He was larger than life and his charisma and influence went beyond the brilliance of his piano-playing, the originality of his compositions, and the compulsion of his continuous love affairs with women and the church. Liszt remained forever the child born in the year of the great planet, for whom the gypsies had foretold the most dazzling future.

It all began with Liszt developing into a child prodigy, captivating everyone with his piano-playing, including Beethoven who is reported to have jumped onto the stage and kissed the child. The piano, of course, remained the heart of Liszt and his soul too, and he was arguably the greatest pianist the world has ever seen. Fortunately, he left behind many pupils whose recordings testify to the brilliance of the master. Piano-playing also won for him the most fantastic fan-following. Women went crazy over Liszt, not only when he was young but also in his old age. He was nearly shot by one admirer; another stripped the covering off a chair on which he had been sitting and hung it on the wall in a frame. Women would surround him while he played and pluck out his hair with special tweezers. One elderly lady obtained the stump of Liszt's cigar and kept it in her bosom for 25 years!

That women would drive him mad was also foretold for Liszt. His father warned him. Liszt turned to God, but God didn't always help. From his childhood, Liszt had been steeped in religion. His favourite reading matter was the Bible. It was so till the end of his days when he became an abbé. But the church couldn't keep the women from his door. This is the great Lisztian romantic contradiction. His affairs were more difficult to count than the warts that grew on his face in his old age. Of his two most famous affairs, one was with the Countess Maria d'Agoult who gave him two daughters and a son. One of the daughters was Cosima, who married Richard Wagner. The second affair was

Liszt travels in his old age dressed as an abbé, by Batt.

with the Russian princess Carolyne who almost succeeded in marrying Liszt. In between, there were affairs with the exotic Lola Montez and the liberated George Sand.

A fabulous life, perhaps only possible in the Romantic Age. But what about the music? Is listening to Liszt as exciting as reading about his life? The answer is a definite 'yes', and what's more, through his championship of Wagner, Liszt encouraged Wagner to continue composing, thus helping the music world gain many treasures. Liszt was perhaps even more unique as a musician than as a man.

Let us first deal with Wagner's debt to Liszt. Not only did Liszt help Wagner by conducting his music when no one looked at him, but he actually showed Wagner the way to compose new music. Liszt was primarily a piano composer and a pianist, but he secretly composed orchestral music. (Now, they are, of course, no longer a secret, but in the Romantic Age, no one wanted to hear the other Liszt.) These orchestral tone poems, as they came to be called, Liszt showed to Wagner. Wagner was fascinated and he further enriched and developed them into his great orchestral style. Liszt didn't mind and gladly helped Wagner. In fact, the only time they fell out was when Wagner stole Liszt's daughter Cosima away from her husband. After Wagner's death, Liszt continued to preach the Wagnerian philosophy.

Although Liszt was a brilliantly innovative orchestral composer and composed many suites, tone poems and two exotic symphonies, one on Faust and the other on Dante, he is primarily remembered as a composer of the piano. This is not surprising, for Liszt's piano music is astoundingly beautiful and varied. Start with the two piano concertos, which are moods crystallized in music. One is serene and contemplative, and the other, raging and tempestuous. After the heroic first and the poetic second piano concertos, come to his solo piano music. Liszt set almost everything to the piano, from abstract concepts like 'benediction' and 'consolation' to concrete descriptions of places. It is best to divide his piano music into two categories—the original creations and the transcriptions. In the category of original creations, try the astounding *Transcendental Etudes* and the *Années de Pelerinage* (Years of Pilgrimage), and masterpieces like *Liebesträum* (Love Dreams) and the *Hungarian Rhapsodies*. Of course, you cannot miss the glorious Sonata in B Minor, perhaps the most important sonata composed in the Romantic era. The second part of *Années* is on *Italie* and is particularly significant from the point of view of the Romantic Age as it is inspired by the poems of Petrarch, Dante and the paintings of Raphael. It is very typical of romantic music that it exists in conjunction with literature and paintings. From the category of transcriptions, try the opera transcriptions from Rossini, Verdi and Mozart, as also the songs of Schubert.

Lisztomania notwithstanding, Liszt was more than just a showman. He was an amazing phenomenon without whose charismatic presence the music world would have been sadly incomplete. Alas, he left no recordings of his amazing piano performances. His music remains—sometimes a consolation, sometimes a stimulation, always a message of great beauty and power.

The Quintessential Romantic

Romantic Age made composers as also their music increasingly complex. Gone were the days of the Bachs who, for generations, were composers to whom music came naturally—they were simple and God-fearing, dedicating their music to the Almighty.

Consider Robert Schumann (1810-1856), born a year after Mendelssohn. Recently, a pianist brought out an album of Schumann's piano music, whose sleeve notes consisted of a play where two characters—both psychologists—discuss the mind and madness of Robert Schumann. The music is presented as a reflection of a mental condition. Each movement, as it were, is akin to the removal of a mask. While this might be an extreme example of trying to link music to life, even if it is a 'romantic' life, there cannot be any doubt that Schumann composed in a very unique manner, unlike any other composer, and that his music is linked very closely to his life, companions and friends.

It is now believed that Schumann's madness was hereditary. His father was mentally ill and so were his aunts. He had periods of vivid sanity, and was arguably the most scholarly of all composers, respected for his learning by none lesser than Johannes Brahms. Schumann loved a beautiful woman and was passionately loved in return by the lovely young pianist, Clara Wieck. They eventually married and had seven children.

Yet one night, at the age of 46, Schumann jumped into the river Rhine. He was rescued and put into an asylum where he lived for two years. Never again did he compose a bar of music, and spent his days making a list of the cities of the world. There was no apparent reason why he should have been so unhappy. Yet he was. Psychologists have spent lifetimes analyzing the cause of Schumann's madness. Perhaps it was the curse of romanticism, the same curse that destroyed the marvellous painter Casper David Friedrich.

Schumann was a dedicated romantic, the man who could write great music and prose at the same time. With Schumann began the brotherhood of composers. His pen discovered for the world two great composers—

Portrait of Schumann.

Chopin and Brahms—and his music makes writers like Jean Paul Richter come to life even today. Schumann's role as a music critic is not often appreciated. For many years he edited a music magazine and opened doors to the appreciation of modern music. He rediscovered Schubert, for much of Schubert's music, including the *Unfinished* and *The Great C Major* symphonies, suffered gross neglect after his death. It was Robert Schumann who brought Schubert back to a new generation.

Ultimately, it is Schumann's music that makes him immortal. His pen may have helped his fellow composers and indirectly posterity as well. His personal tragedy may have hurt Clara and destroyed a happy family, but in the end there is his music, the *Traumerei* (Dreams) for piano which can add new life to a TV commercial; the wonderful piano suites—*Carnaval, Kreisleriana* and *Kinderszenen* (of which the *Traumerei* is a part), the glorious *Fantasie* (Fantasy) in C Major in which he wrote the last word on the Romantic piano sonata, the piano concerto, the cello concerto, the symphonies and songs.

His manner of composition could provide us with a clue to his mind. Schumann composed in bursts. No other composer in the world of music was given to impulse as Schumann was. In his period of songs, he was obsessed with songs and nothing else. During this period he composed the famous *Frauenliebe und Leben* (woman's life and love) in which he wrote about his life and death even before his marriage. His chamber music period saw him composing the miraculous piano quintet, the piano quartet and the string quartets; in his symphonic phase, he composed

Schumann with his wife Clara.

his famous *Spring* Symphony commemorating his marriage in music, and in his concerto phase came the exquisite piano concerto, the somber cello concerto, and the violin concerto, which Clara Schumann withheld from publication as she did not think it good enough for Schumann. It has been played and recorded after World War II. This creative method of obsessive concentration has no parallel in music.

Schumann remains a neglected composer, almost a musician's musician. His four symphonies are performed regularly, but it is his piano music that tantalizes and attracts all great pianists. Discover it for yourself. For like the man who was so different, his piano sings with a voice that is unique, reviving as it were the life and times of a great romantic.

Chopin—The Poet of Peace

all the composers included in the pantheon of greats, the one I turn to most when I need peace of mind is Fryderyk Chopin (1810-1849). For me, nothing evokes the state of joyous peacefulness like a Chopin nocturne[1], or the bacarolle[2] and the berceuse[3], the two compositions always paired together. They suggest sleep—gentle, lovely sleep.

I have been reading *Chopin's Funeral* by Benita Eisler. The book is about Chopin's life and music and provides some rare insights. Chopin's life and music of intense passion makes one terribly sorry for the man who, like Keats, was a hopeless consumptive. Today, the study of Chopin as a creative individual is highly relevant in an era where creativity in relation to exile/diaspora—loss of identity, the artist living away from his roots, the displaced individual, concerns us greatly. Chopin was an exile, the quintessential displaced artist. He was born a wheelwright's son in Poland and at 20, left for Vienna and later Paris where he lived till his death. Chopin's extravagant ways, the dozens of pairs of expensive gloves for which he had a fetish, the expensive wines, flowers and apartments, hiring a private coach, valet and coachmen, were all an attempt to forge an identity away from home.

He was on first name terms with royalty and had George Sand, then the most famous woman in Paris, as his mistress. Ironically, when he died, Sand and Chopin had separated and she did not attend his funeral. But Solange, her daughter, with whom Chopin had developed a very touching relationship, was there.

[1] *Nocturne* or *Nocherne* refers to Night pieces; also referred to at times as *Nachtmusik* by Mahler and *Notturno* by Schubert.

[2] Boat songs.

[3] To rock or to sleep to a lullaby.

Chopin leaves his last concert, 18 November, 1848, London. By Batt.

Illustration of a Chateaubriand book. Writer-politician Chateaubriand had a strong influence on the romantic composers and was an admirer of Chopin's music.

The funeral was magnificent: 'Crowds poured into the square in front of the Church of the Madeleine and the entire façade of the great neoclassical temple had been draped in swathes of black velvet, centred with a cartouche bearing the silver-embroidered initials of the composer. Admission was by invitation only: between three and four thousand had received the black-bordered cards.' London had rejected Chopin when the composer visited the city a year before his death. He longed for a royal concert, but Queen Victoria was not interested. But *The Times,* London, sent a music critic to write about the funeral.

The affair between Sand and Chopin was a crucial relationship. From Chopin's early indifference to their final quarrel, and the composer's sadness over the final separation was one of the greatest of romantic affairs. Consider the opening theme of the sonata for piano and cello based on the first song of Schubert's song-cycle *Winterreise:* 'A stranger I am and a stranger I depart.' Chopin who otherwise hardly ever mentions Schubert, was obsessed with this song that reflected his identity crisis and central tragedy. When August Franchomme, the cellist and a great friend of Chopin, inspired him to compose his only sonata which uses an instrument other than the piano, Chopin quoted from this song. In his last concert in Paris, the sonata was presented with Franchomme playing the cello and Chopin himself on the piano. But Chopin omitted the first movement that had the *Winterreise* quotation.

Chopin had thought that the quotation from Schubert would be understood by the very knowledgeable crowd who would link it to the tragedy of a broken relationship. Sand was to Chopin a pillar of strength. Take the Valldemosa interlude. Chopin and Sand were visiting Majorca in search of sunshine. But Chopin's health suddenly deteriorated and he started coughing blood. Majorca was worried about infection and banished the couple to a monastery, Valldemosa, on a hilltop. The story of how Sand, just to enable Chopin to compose and play the piano, managed to get a piano from Paris, and have it moved up the hill is quite extraordinary: 'Sand had to arrange to transport this delicate mechanism with its hundreds of moveable parts over the five inaccessible miles of mountain roads...its delivery, intact and even in tune from an unsprung cart could only be explained as a miracle performed by Chopin's guardian angel.'

Chopin was a brilliant teacher and developed a unique rapport with the brilliant young pianist Karl Filtisch, who also died of consumption. They played a two-piano arrangement of Chopin's E Minor piano concerto. A report says: 'On the evening of the concert, the duet of teacher and pupil emerged as an apostolic succession, the 13-year-old's delicacy and sureness of touch a worthy tribute to the master who evoked from memory the entire orchestra.'

Three doctors came to treat Chopin in Majorca. 'One said I am going to die, the second that I am dying, the third that I was already dead,' wrote Chopin. About his own predicament and loss of identity Chopin once said, 'I am like a cobweb for whom all the walls have crumbled.' Charles Halle found Chopin 'hardly able to move, bent like a half-opened pen-knife and evidently in great pain.' He insisted, nonetheless, upon playing for his guests. He had promised, and he hated pleading illness.

His guests were relieved to see that 'as he warmed to his work, his body gradually resumed its normal position, the spirit having mastered the flesh.'

Chopin's musical compositions—nocturnes, preludes, etudes, mazurkas, polonaises, waltzes and fantasies (eternal symbols of the triumph of the human spirit over the vulnerability of the human body)—live on.

Liszt's mistress Maria d'Agoult once remarked that the only constant thing about Chopin was his cough. This statement rather pathetically sums up the trials of the consumptive composer who died at 39, mourning the fact that he could not breathe his last in his beloved Poland. Later, however, Chopin's heart was cut out from his body and taken for burial to his homeland.

Ironically, although it was a well-known fact that Chopin was suffering from infectious tuberculosis, it did not prevent him from conducting a continuous series of affairs with women, including the famous one with George Sand, which lasted the longest. His love life defies logic and could well have hastened his early death. More logical is his music—structured, precise and classical. Indeed, it is not often appreciated that though Chopin is one of the enduring symbols of the Romantic Age, his music was classical in its restraint and purity. In this, he differs from his great contemporary Liszt. A literary simile helps in clarifying the fundamental difference between Chopin and Liszt. Chopin was classically controlled like Keats, while Liszt was at times like the wild west wind that was Shelley.

The centre of Chopin's life was Paris, his adopted home where he returned again and again from his travels, and where he died. In Paris, he was right at the heart of a circle of great people: Delacroix the painter, Balzac, Liszt, Mendelssohn, Lamartine and Berlioz. There were others like Saint-Beuve, Victor Hugo and Chateaubriand, who formed the private circle of his listeners. Chopin hated public concerts and gave only a few throughout his life. He was intensely nervous and the mention of public concerts would drive him to a pathological state.

Chopin was very friendly with the painter Delacroix. The great artist painted a famous portrait of Chopin at the piano and Sand, cigar in hand, standing beside the piano. Later, long after Chopin's death, the canvas was cut into two and now the two portraits are housed in two different museums. Delacroix was a regular visitor at Nohant, Sand's country estate outside Paris and liked listening to Chopin playing Beethoven sonatas. Although Chopin's favourites were Mozart and Bach, his playing of Beethoven left Delacroix spellbound. Chopin's favourite painter, however, was not Delacroix, but Ingres, a preference that confirms Chopin was a classicist and not a romantic in spirit.

He was at his best in private recitals, and the little group of poets, painters and intellectuals in Paris forming a crescent around the remarkable George Sand, heard many of his compositions for the first time, works that are iconic today. Chopin's nervousness and diffidence are sometimes reflected in his music which can best be described as the gentle breeze that blows across a secluded garden at night.

Even when Chopin is angry, as in his famous *Revolutionary Etude* and his polonaises, it is a civilized anger, the tantrum of a basically gentle, mild-mannered person. I have always believed that Chopin is the ideal composer for the tropics, as his music is cooling, gentle and refreshing—a unique quality that astounds us, given that he was always so horribly ill. Very often, when Chopin was composing, he could hardly breathe—yet there was no trace of pain or sorrow in his music.

His creative voice sublimates the physical, and words such as 'sublime' and 'angelic' come again and again to mind. No wonder Chopin has been accepted so completely by everybody. After Bach, Beethoven and Mozart, he is perhaps the most popular composer. For many, he is synonymous with music. Yet he composed primarily for only two musical instruments—the piano and the cello. Genius, like love, defies logic.

Where do we begin with Chopin? Perhaps with his chamber music, for there is so little. Listen to the hauntingly beautiful Cello Sonata, followed by the *Polonaise Brillante* for cello and piano. Next, try his polonaises and mazurkas, the two forms that sometimes link Chopin with the Nationalists. The mazurka is based on a Polish folk dance, and much of the polonaises use Polish melodies. Chopin loved his homeland and never stopped regretting the fact that he was an exile. Listening to these easily comprehensible pieces gives you the feel of essential Chopin. After this, try the First Piano Concerto, which has some glorious melodies and a wonderful love-haunted slow movement, and the Second Piano Sonata with the great funeral march. You are now ready to explore the world of Chopin which consists of waltzes, preludes, etudes, ballades, scherzos and the incomparable nocturnes. Chopin's nocturnes are like the most haunting perfume of Arabia frozen into melody.

He also wrote a series of Fantasies which are, justifiably, very popular. In churning out melodies, Chopin was a close second to Schubert. It is not surprising that many of Chopin's melodies have been turned into songs in the 20th century. Unlike the pronunciation of his name, about which no two people agree, there is no second opinion about the greatness of Chopin.

Contemporary caricature of George Sand.

TIME, LIGHT AND MUSIC

Does Western classical music have any connection with the time of the day like its Indian counterpart? Well, the question is so complex that a simple 'yes' or 'no' will not do. Let me say straightaway that Western classical music does not have anything like early morning ragas, late afternoon ragas and late night ragas—*Asavari, Lalit, Marwa, Malkauns* and *Darbari*—but it does have an intimate, almost spiritual connection with the journey of the day towards the night.

One of the earliest examples of this is the concept of the 'Vigil' and church singing throughout the night till the break of dawn. This is especially true of the Russian Orthodox tradition. Although the history of this art form goes back to the earliest times, the end of the 19th century finds both Rachmaninoff and Tchaikovsky writing music in this ancient form. Indeed the Church is a very good starting point to understand the link between music and the time of the day.

The Matin, for instance, is the prayer for the morning and composers have written music for this time as they have done for the evening Vespers. Mozart, Bach and Vivaldi wrote many Vespers. The composer Joseph Haydn tried to translate a Church concept into symphonic music early in his career with his famous *Times of Day* symphonies known as *Matin, Midi, Soir* (morning, afternoon, evening). He was fully aware that the community for whom he was composing would be aware of the Church conventions and would relate to these symphonies. They are in fact evocative and one of the first examples of mood music—a concept perfected in the late 19th century.

The conductor Helmut Muller-Bruhl feels that in the second of these symphonies, Haydn approaches the kind of atmosphere created by the painter Tintoretto in his afternoon landscapes. If you listen to these symphonies carefully you will feel the joy of the morning, the languidness of the afternoon and the mystery of approaching twilight. Before Haydn, Vivaldi had created similar music and time connections in his *Four Seasons,* where he evokes the mood of a summer afternoon through the lazy cooing of the dove and the drunken stupor of the peasant.

Before Chopin, Wagner and Mahler, Joseph Haydn was perhaps the greatest exponent of linking the time of the day to music. He wrote a string quartet called *Sunrise,* which evokes the mood of early morning. Beethoven did it more subtly in the introduction to his Fourth Symphony, which he said represented the light of the early morning. He in fact specified the time as 4 a.m. If Beethoven is to be taken at his word, he was doing for listeners what the *Raga Bhairon* does for Indian classical music.

Before I come to the 19th-century Romantic composer's involvement with day moving towards night, a word about the tone and colour of instruments. In his tone poem, *Also Sprach Zarathustra,* Richard Strauss suggests the dazzling brilliance of sunlight with an ecstatic outpouring of brass music—horns, trombones and trumpets. Although the poet Keats wrote of the 'silver snarling trumpets', the brass section suggests gold more than silver. I equate sunrise and daylight with music that has a lot of brass. On the other hand the bassoon and bass clarinet, particularly in the lower registers, as in the utterly traumatized beginning of the *Pathetique*, suggests the soul of the night and the darkest gloom and despair. That is the mood that Tchaikovsky sets in his tone poem, *Francesca da Rimini.*

The cello always suggests various shades of brown, a study in ennui, contemplation and emotions recollected in tranquility. The finest example of this occurs in the third movement of Brahms' Second Piano Concerto. If Rembrandt could play a musical instrument, he would have played the cello. The cello sound is like a Rembrandt painting, a haunting interplay of light and darkness. The clarinet sound as depicted by Mozart in his incomparable concerto is deep purple, haunting and enigmatic like the approaching twilight. Here the time of the day is a personal choice, but the clarinet concerto of Mozart is certainly the *Raga Marwa* of Western classical music, to be played in the twilight zone.

Both Keats and Mozart made a pact with death. Though Mozart was not strictly a Romantic, this aspect of his character is very close to Keats' utterance of being 'half in love with easeful death'. Thus it was that the Romantic composers—from Chopin composing those exquisite capsule night fragrances which he called nocturnes, to Mahler's *nachtmusik* in his Seventh Symphony and Wagner's heartbreaking 'Liebestod' in *Tristan and Isolde,* and longing for the night—made music move through a clear-cut process in time. A Chopin nocturne is like taking a walk in a garden at night with all the myriad known and unknown floral scents. Chopin, except for his mazurkas and polonaises, composed almost exclusively for the night. There is also hardly any day music in Mahler except perhaps the earth-shattering hymn of praise at the beginning of the *Symphony of a Thousand.* In the second movement of the same symphony, he goes back into the deep, dark night with music that suggests a nocturnal procession of pilgrims very close to what Mendelssohn portrayed in the *Italian* Symphony. Verdi's music has the richness of dark velvet. When Verdi does suggest light, it is the colour generated by fire burning in the forest, as in *Il Trovatore. Rigoletto* is almost entirely played out in the dark and the only light that dazzles is that emerging from the chandeliers in the duke's court. Wagner's *Tristan* suggests a deep understanding of the spirit of the night. Ironically, when he does suggest light, as in the brilliant *Tannhauser* overture, Wagner creates the illusion of fireworks like Handel did more obviously in the *Music for the Royal Fireworks*.

The Romantics are easier to classify into night and day with the scale weighing heavily towards night. But it is more ambivalent with the Classical and Baroque masters. Take Bach. His cantatas were all written to be performed at certain periods of the day depending on the timings of the church service. But the music is not specifically linked to the time of the day. However, his *Goldberg* Variations are certainly written to be played at night, originally composed to put an insomniac Duke to sleep. Beethoven's *Pastoral* gives a clear idea of the time, which is linked with the daily routine of the shepherds. But such cases are rare. The choice ultimately depends on the listener's response and the mood of the music.

Troika

Refreshing as a Mountain Spring

ever a composer was surprised that he could compose music, it was Antonin Dvorak (1841-1904). He once said, 'I learnt music from birds, leaves, flowers, stars and God.' After Schubert, he was the most naturally gifted composer. His music will surprise you with its spontaneity, freshness and joy. A simple peasant at heart, Dvorak retained the unspoilt pleasure of the simple rustic life in his melodies. The childlike Dvorak was a great friend of two highly sophisticated men—Brahms and Tchaikovsky. Both were great admirers of Dvorak's music. Brahms said of Dvorak's Cello Concerto that if he knew it was possible to compose like that for the cello, he would have done so long ago.

If a competition was to be held among composers you would love to meet, Dvorak would probably win hands down. He was a rustic, loving person who couldn't harm a soul. He was fond of animals, particularly pigs and pigeons, and he adored railway engines.

When not involved in composing a symphony, he would travel down to the nearest station and watch the trains come in, note down the engine numbers and make friends with the drivers. In fact, they were his best friends. Railway engines do not appear in his compositions in any obvious manner, but he celebrated the pigeons in his famous slow movement of the G Major symphony where the strings simulate the organized flight of pigeons making for the sky. It is a glorious innovation.

Though naive, Dvorak did not lack common sense. He did not end up making a mess of his affairs like Mozart who was otherwise such a sophisticated person. Dvorak understood his worth as a composer and dealt with his publishers with great acumen. The result was that he was able to buy a dream villa in Bohemia, and make several trips to London and New York. Like composers before him—Handel, Haydn, Mozart,

Mendelssohn and Weber—Dvorak was a great success in London, and today, a century later, his popularity in the city has in no way diminished. Some of the greatest Dvorak recordings have been by the English orchestras.

In New York, he was probably a greater success, and America must be thanked for inspiring Dvorak to create two of his greatest works—the *New World* Symphony and the *American* Quartet. Both were Dvorak's reactions on listening to Black spirituals. The symphony must surely rank as one of the most popular symphonies in the repertoire, but the quartet too is exquisite.

There is hardly a dull bar in Dvorak, so it is difficult to make a recommended listening list of his music. Perhaps a good way to begin would be with the Cello Concerto. This is without doubt the greatest cello concerto ever composed. It has wonderful soaring melodies for the cello, and a ravishing slow movement. Almost all great cellists have recorded it, but the two most cherished recordings are by Pablo Casals and Jacqueline du Pre. The Cello Concerto has somewhat obscured Dvorak's Violin Concerto, but that too is a lovely work.

After the concertos, we come to his two serenades—the one for strings and the other for wind instruments, and the Slavonic Dances, both the two piano and the orchestral versions. It is with this music that Dvorak made all his money.

The Dvorak symphony is something special. It seems to blend elements of Schubert and Bruckner with an orchestration and melodic richness all its own. The *New World* dominates the cycle, but listen to the G Major and D Minor symphonies as well. The latter is regarded by many as his greatest symphony. Dvorak was a wonderful composer of chamber music, and wrote in almost all the possible combinations. He used the Czech dance form known as the *dumka,* and the best-known work using this form is his *Dumky* trio for cello, piano and violin. The op. 81 piano quintet and the string quartets and quintets are also beautiful compositions.

With the arrival of Dvorak in the second half of the 19th century, Czechoslovakia entered permanently the map of European classical music. Of course, there was Jan Dismas Zelenka (1679-1745) before, but Zelenka is being discovered only recently. Before Dvorak, Czechoslovakia was a place where only Mozart travelled often. But Dvorak changed all that. Today, his symphonies, concertos and chamber music are some of the best-loved compositions.

The Tragic Loner

Some of music's strangest controversies revolve around Pyotr Tchaikovsky (1840-1893). Some concern his life, others his music. A few years ago, Ken Russell made a film on his life which somewhat superficially dwelt on his homosexuality, without analyzing the torment and agony it caused him or exploring how it was reflected in his music. Even today, more than a century after his death, people continue to discuss Tchaikovsky's last moments. Did he die of cholera after drinking unboiled water or did he kill himself after the premiere of his world-famous *Pathetique* Symphony? The truth will perhaps never be known with absolute certainty. But there's no doubt his music, particularly the last three symphonies, and the piano and violin concertos, remain great vintage pieces of the concert hall, never mind what some say about his offerings being too sweet. Even today, we haven't begun to understand the tragedy of his life.

The composer's unusual life spans his short and disastrous marriage, his long friendship with a woman he never met, his many attempts at suicide and his manic depressive temperament. There are several biographies for those interested. Tchaikovsky is, in fact, a favourite with biographers. One minute his melodies smile and the next, a strange dissonance plunges the proceedings into despair and gloom. For most people, Tchaikovsky is the creator of those world-famous ballets—*Sleeping Beauty, Swan Lake* and *The Nutcracker*. They are fabulous fun and contain some of his most memorable music. Indeed, no music dances the way Tchaikovsky's does, not only in his ballets, but also in his concertos and symphonies. Though the waltz is synonymous with Johann Strauss, it is Tchaikovsky who gave it symphonic status, weaving into his symphonies some of the most mysterious waltzes ever composed.

The best way to make friends with Tchaikovsky is through his First Piano Concerto in B flat Minor. It is spine-chilling music, and recordings by pianists like Horowitz or Claudio Arrau, are an experience of a lifetime. The memorable theme of the first movement

Tchaikovsky broods, by Batt.

Da Capo
Coda

The score of a page from the Pathetique *Symphony.*

comes from the song of a blind lyre-player and singer whom the composer had heard. In fact, the whole concerto sings, and the second movement too uses the refrain of an old French song which Tchaikovsky and his brother used to sing as children. The brilliant third movement has been compared to a Cossack dance. The opening theme of this great piano concerto was used by Charlie Chaplin as the background music for his film *Limelight*. If Tchaikovsky had written nothing else but this concerto and the *Pathetique* Symphony, he would have secured a place amongst the immortals of music. Fortunately, however, he wrote a lot more, like the glorious and luminous Violin Concerto, which is full of gracious melodies and is a favourite with all violinists.

Come now to the Fourth and Fifth symphonies of the master. The Fourth begins with an astonishing fanfare for brass which opens a work of amazing brilliance. Many consider this his greatest symphony, though the composer's own favourite was the *Pathetique*. The Fourth was written in the aftermath of his near-fatal marriage to Antonina Milyukova, and carries the mental and emotional upsets which scarred Tchaikovsky at this time. It is a programmatic work based on the idea of the final triumph of the artist over an adverse fate. Quite ironically, Tchaikovsky dedicated this symphony, which was born out of his disastrous relationship with one woman, to the other in his life, his patron, Madame von Meck, whom he was never to meet. Whatever else you listen to of Tchaikovsky, don't forget the *Pizzicato Ostinato* (Plucked Strings), the third movement of this symphony. Symphony no. 5 in E Minor was written by a considerably older and more mature Tchaikovsky. It reveals a sense of resignation with his lot, and a simple affirmation of his new-found faith. This deeply felt music, full of melancholy passion and yearning, comes from an emotional equilibrium new to Tchaikovsky. The waltz in this symphony is much like all the flowers and fairies in this world dancing together.

Tchaikovsky's last symphony, the *Pathetique,* is, in a way, a trendsetter. The slow movement is put as the finale, which was unprecedented. (To end a symphony with a slow movement is rare. Hayden did it once in the *Farewell,* Symphony no. 45, and after Tchaikovsky, Mahler did it in the Ninth Symphony.) The *Pathetique* is a dark and despairing symphony—a vivid expression of Tchaikovsky's emotional suffering in the year leading up to his death. The composer's brother Modest gave the symphony its title by which it is known in the musical world. The first movement is an invocation of darkness from the lowest depths. The second, as Modest wrote, 'dwells on the fleeting joys of my brother's life'. The third movement is the spookiest music you will ever hear, and is like two skeletons dancing a waltz that is macabre and haunting. The last movement is a slow dirge and justifies Tchaikovsky's claim of calling his Sixth Symphony his requiem.

The Soul of Rocks

rugged rocks and fjords of Finland found their voice in the music of Jean Sibelius, one of the greatest landscape painters in music. When the composer of Finland's national anthem 'Finlandia' died in 1957 at the age of 92, he was regarded as the last titan of classical music. The composer of seven symphonies, a great violin concerto and mysterious tone poems based on the rugged contours and the numerous legends and lore of the land, Sibelius for some unaccountable reason went silent in 1925 after composing the tone poem *Tapiola.* For thirty years, Sibelius was a musical monolith with his monumental bald head which critics feel inspired Bergman's vision of death in the film *Seventh Seal.* Patiently the musical world waited for an eighth symphony. But the rest was silence. Sibelius was not the only composer who suddenly stopped composing. In the 19th century there was Rossini, who at the age of 37, after the composition of the opera *William Tell* withdrew from the world of opera. But he at least composed some chamber music and religious music in his old age. Sibelius, however remained stubbornly silent though from his home in a log cabin in Finland, he gave countless interviews, met visitors and aspiring musicians spreading rumours about a new symphony. But only sketches exist and the mystery of the Sibelian silence will never be solved.

A gaunt and rugged tree spreading its leafless branches like a hand with twisted fingers. The death of nature, frozen and embalmed—that is the image that Sibelius's *Tapiola,* based on an ancient mythical God, and the violin concerto brings to mind. The concerto ranks with the greatest in the genre: Beethoven, Brahms, Mendelssohn and Tchaikovsky. And *Tapiola* is like some sleeping giant regaining consciousness after centuries of sleep. Both works are masterpieces that will remain favourites with conductors and violinists.

Where do you begin with Sibelius? Perhaps with *Finlandia,* Sibelius's most famous work. Listening to it for the first time can create quite an impact. The orchestration is different. The sound is different. This

Sibelius stands in front of his home in Helsinki.

is like no other music. In a famous meeting with Mahler, the two composers discussed their symphonies. Mahler said that his symphony was the universe. It contained everything like a vast endless mural. Sibelius said, 'my symphonies are the essence of concentration, a microcosm of sound that gives the distilled essence the soul of life.' This impression is contained in what are arguably the two greatest of his symphonies, the Fourth and the Fifth. The Fourth evokes haunting scenes, like a graveyard covered by fog. Composed during World War I, it is like the desolate landscape paintings of Paul Nash.

Sibelius's method of composition is very unusual. His music sounds like several tonal fragments. Slowly these fragments come together as the music progresses and a theme is born. It is like one of those puzzles with shapes. When all the shapes fit together you get a complete picture. This is the feeling that the one movement Seventh gives, a symphony that is like an abstract landscape made of wisps of clouds, mists and haze. A landscape in tones, whose only equivalent are the paintings of Turner.

Sibelius was certainly the most important symphonist since Brahms. His sound world is extraordinary and his music is unlike that of any other European composer, like a massive black rock which has suddenly found a voice.

The universality of western classical music is evident in that it can contain within its ambience two such different symphonies as Mahler's *Symphony of the Thousands* and the sparse and epigrammatic Fourth Symphony of Sibelius. The great music and cricket writer, Neville Cardus, described the Fourth as a 'googly' with which Sibelius baffled the music world. It is perhaps the strangest of all symphonies, the requiem of a civilization confronting change. In the sad and wistful slow movement of this path-breaking work, you can actually see flowers blooming on a cactus; life erupting out of a deathly silence. The Fifth Symphony is even more stunning. The most unexpected moment in symphonic music comes in the closing bars of this symphony. Sibelius builds up a massive climax, tone upon tone, sound upon sound, and then suddenly the music is axed like an executioner chopping off one's head.

BIRDS AND BEES

The Catalogue of Birds by Oliver Messiaen (1908-1992) is surely one of the most unusual works of music ever created. I have always wanted to listen to this vast pianistic panorama of bird songs, and now a recording has come into my collection, thanks to a musical brother belonging to the rare monastic community of Taize in France.

I remember listening to Messiaen's *Tarangalila* Symphony long ago and being bowled over by it. It was written at a time (1946-1948) when the symphonic tradition seemed at its lowest ebb. The music blended elements of Shostakovich and Mahler on an epic scale, seeking to embrace the totality of the human experience. This is implied in the Sanskrit title and Messiaen's interest in Indian music.

Messiaen was a brilliant teacher, who nurtured the talents of composers like Iannis Xenakis, Pierre Boulez and Karlheinz Stockhausen. He was also a deeply religious composer who believed that music transports us to God: 'I have tried to be a Christian musician and put my faith into a song,' he said.

His engagement with the *Catalogue of Birds* (1956-1958) turned Messiaen into an ornithological expert. An interest developed since the age of 15 had led to an exhaustive in-depth study. He was like a modern-day St. Francis of Assisi in the field at all hours of the day and night, taking dictations from his winged-masters whom he liked to call 'the greatest musicians on our planet'. The music is minimal and, at times, reminiscent of Satie, Webern and Hindemith. But the sonic effect is fascinating. He creates through the piano a musical manifestation of nature which he calls 'an inexhaustible treasury of sounds and colours, shapes and rhythms—a peerless model of total evolution and endless variety. Nature is the supreme resource.'

In Messiaen's obsession with winged creatures is reflected music's long link with bird songs, their flights and the grace, elegance and beauty of one of nature's most inspired creations. It's not just musical instruments—singers too simulate bird songs. Coloratura sopranos are judged by their closeness to birdcalls. Jenny Lind, the famous soprano, was known as the Swedish nightingale. Piccolos and flutes warble like birds. The Vivaldi piccolo concerto is like a continuous stream of bird songs, drawing out a string of fascinating melodies. In his suicidal note, *The Heiligenstadt Testament,* Beethoven mourned that he could not hear the songs of birds because of his deafness.

Take a work like Johnannes Brahms' Clarinet Quintet, which reminded Neville Cardus of a nightingale tossing lovely notes on the summer air: 'And the solo clarinet sings like a bird in a dark forest; the strings make the soft murmurs of leaves and trees in the night—it is a nightingale; listen especially to the low notes. Listen carefully to the lovely way that Brahms makes the strings sway and nestle round the solo clarinet and the solo gradually dies drowsily down like a bird moving towards slumber, and we are left in the deep silence of the wood when the music comes to an end.' Traditionally, we think of the piccolo and the flute as being close to bird calls, but here Cardus is speaking of the clarinet.

If Messiaen's deeply resonant piano is any indication, the bassoon and even the tuba can remind us of birds!

Composers have consciously tried to incorporate bird songs, bird calls and bird flights into their music. Sometimes, they did this with a touch of humour, as Couperin did in his harpsichord piece, *The Poule.* Haydn added a bit of fun by incorporating a sound similar to that of a clucking hen in the second subject of the first movement of his Symphony no. 83 in G Minor, from which the symphony got its name. One of the most famous bird work is Handel's Organ Concerto in G Minor—*The Cuckoo and the Nightingale*. The concerto gets its name from the bird song motifs of the second movement. Handel's organ concertos were written as fillers to be played during the intermissions of his mighty oratorios and operas. Handel himself often played the solo instrument. Although only the G Minor concerto got this nickname, most of the 16 concertos sound like the calls of birds when played on a small, portable organ.

Mozart was inspired by birds too. In his Piano Concerto in G Major (K 453), the last movement simulates the songs of his pet canary. Birds are all over *The Magic Flute*. Papageno, the bird catcher, moves around with a cage of birds and makes his flute sound like bird songs. The mind of the listener is never far from the birds during this magic opera.

One of the most imaginative simulations of bird life is Joseph Haydn's String Quartet, *The Lark,* op. 64, no. 5. In the first movement of this lovely work, Haydn, through the violin's soaring melody, simulates the upward flight of the lark. Something similar happens in the violin caprice, *The Lark Ascending,* by the composer Vaughan Williams. The work is significantly dated 1914—the year of the war that was to silence many an English lark. The music is prefaced by the following quotation from a poem by George Meredith:

He rises and begins to round
He drops the silver chain of sound
Of many links without a break
In chirrup, whistle, slur and shake...
Till lost on his aerial rings
In light, and then the fancy sings.

Vaughan Williams's *The Lark Ascending* is truly a fantasia for violin and orchestra, a 'soundscape' that offers an aural comment on this poem.

Bird sounds have been used rather uniquely in Wagner's opera *Siegfried*. The woodbird, sung by a soprano, leads the hero to the cave of the dragon, guarding the treasure of the Ring. Like most composers, Wagner made the soprano simulate the bird calls. A coloratura roll rings through the forest, haunting and eerie in its warbling.

In Dvorak's Symphony no. 8, the second movement, the adagio, suggests the upward movement of pigeons in flight. As one hears this haunting music, one recalls that Dvorak was a pigeon collector and a nature lover. Composers have captured in music the stately movement of birds as Camille Saint-Saëns did in his world-famous *The Swan*.

While on birds, we must not forget the bees. Rimsky Korsakov's *The Flight of the Bumble Bee* is delightful nature music that eternally symbolizes the composer's love of the natural world from which he constantly drew his inspiration.

Wagnerknights

Richard The Great

greatest tragedy of Wagner's life was that he was discovered by Adolf Hitler. Once the word spread that Wagner was Hitler's favourite composer, Wagner's status as a musician and composer came under a cloud. Today, decades after the end of the Great War, the Wagner magic has lost much of its sting except perhaps in the Wagner music festival town, Bayreuth, which remains a place of pilgrimage for Wagnerites. The music world is divided over Wagner. There are those who hate him because he was an anti-Semite and wrote the book *Das Judenthum in der Musik* (Jewry in Music). Ironically, it has been suggested that Wagner may have been the illegitimate son of a Jew, Ludwig Geyer, an actor, and thus himself carried Jewish blood. The Jewish lobby has, understandably, forced Wagner out of many concert halls and record shops. Another group finds Wagner's music loud and vulgar, and his monstrously long operas dull and boring. Finally, there is a group for whom Wagner is one of the greatest of all great composers, and his operas like *The Ring of the Nibelungs, Tristan und Isolde, Parsifal,* and *Lohengrin,* the Holy Grail of music. Somewhere in this welter of controversy, the real Wagner has been lost forever.

The facts are as follows: Richard Wagner (1813-1883) was an obnoxious person and one of the world's greatest megalomaniacs. He had supreme confidence in his own talent and believed himself to be a genius who had to be supported by the world. He had no scruples or morals and was totally dishonest about money. He was in fact the apotheosis of the con man and made a special art out of borrowing money and never repaying it. His biographies make fascinating and somewhat annoying reading, and Ernest Newman's book on Wagner is recommended. Imagine the calibre of a man who tricked two women into marrying him, while continuing a homosexual relationship with a young prince, who financed his dream project of a music festival town. But behind this rather unpleasant human being lived a creative genius.

Wagner and Cosima Wagner.

Portrait of Wagner, by Batt.

Hanslick asks Wagner for the rationale of his music.

He could write his own librettos[1] (the script of the opera which are usually written by someone other than the composer) and he changed the course of the orchestra. Without Wagner, we would not have had that glorious composer Gustav Mahler. Neither would we have had Richard Strauss, Jean Sibelius, Sergei Prokofiev, Dmitri Shostakovich and Arnold Schoenberg. If you like the sound of the grand orchestra, there is nothing more evocative than, for instance, the *Forest Murmurs, Siegfried's Rhine Journey* or *The Ride of the Valkyries*. Without words, Wagner's operas are transmuted into a beautiful stream of seamless orchestral music.

There are also the overtures which have always been favourites in the concert halls: *Tannhauser,* with the music from the orchestra cascading like a waterfall; *The Flying Dutchman,* one of the finest musical picturization of the sea; and *Die Meistersinger von Nurnberg*.

But perhaps the greatest of all Wagner operas is *Parsifal*[2], and not even in Mozart and Brahms, has the clarinet been used with such spiritual agony as in the 'Good Friday' music from this opera. The choruses from this opera are also very moving, as are most Wagnerian choruses, which are an extension of the musical world of the Mozart we find in *The Magic Flute*.

Wagner is a composer for whom the concept of 'highlights' is more suitable, since the complete Wagner is an impractical proposition. There is also a need to assess the composer's true artistic worth. But this is a prickly area which Wagner has himself created with his anti-Semitism.

[1] See Opera—Divine Madness, Chapter 3, p. 165.

[2] Some may disagree and say it is *Tristan*. I love *Tristan* too and it is one opera where the words and the two voices, the tenor Tristan and the soprano Isolde mingle so seamlessly with the orchestra that it is impossible to separate them and have a *Tristan* without words. Sorry, this opera of Wagner you must have the complete version. *Tristan* and *Parsifal* are the two extreme points in which Wagner resonates—body and soul.

A Sublime Mountain

Anton

Bruckner (1824-1896) was a most unusual composer, and a very strange human being. If Sigmund Freud had been given the choice of writing a composer's biography, he would surely have selected Bruckner. Why did Bruckner suffer the way he did—from an innate sense of insecurity, depression, panic, anxiety and an obsession for counting things? Other composers before him, like Schumann, had suffered from mental instability, but Bruckner's is a case that continues to baffle psychologists.

Just as there are many opinions about Bruckner's mental state, his music too evokes intense reactions. There are those for whom a Bruckner symphony is a holy sanctuary to be entered only by the initiated, and others who find his symphonies too long and overblown, and lacking in dramatic content. During his lifetime, which ran parallel to those of Wagner and Brahms, his music enjoyed moderate success because he was unwittingly drawn into a controversy that raged over the music of Wagner and Brahms between two opposite camps. The naive Bruckner was an admirer of Wagner ever since he heard *Tannhauser*. He did not imitate Wagner, but the composer was certainly Bruckner's hero. The score of *Tristan and Isolde* lay open in his music stand from the day he obtained it, and he once stood outside Wagner's cottage just to get a glimpse of his hero. The childlike Bruckner declared his love openly, and this annoyed Brahmsians like the critic Edward Hanslick who declared Bruckner to be a 'swindle'. His anti-Brucknerian criticism made Bruckner totally paranoid, and he told his friends, 'Please don't ever annoy Hanslick for his wrath is terrible and he will completely ruin me.'

At the end of his life, when Bruckner was given a room by the Emperor Francis Joseph at the Belvedere Castle, Bruckner was asked by the emperor if there was anything he could do for him. The composer replied, 'Can't Your Majesty see to it that Hanslick doesn't write so rudely about me?' There was a conductor's ban on Bruckner's works during his life, and when the conductor Hans Richter broke the ban to conduct Bruckner's Fourth Symphony, the Romantic, Bruckner naively put a thaler (the currency then in vogue in Austria) on his palm and said, 'Please go out and have a glass of beer.' Bruckner was really impossible.

It is also impossible to believe today that there was a ban on his symphonies more than a hundred years ago. Today, they are at the peak of popularity. In Great Britain, Bruckner is really popular ever since writers like Neville Cardus and Deryck Cooke sang his praises. The praise was taken up by conductors such as Otto Klemperer, Jascha Horenstein, Eugen Jochum, and more recently, Gunter Wand and Bernard Haitink. A new generation of critics and writers like Richard Osborne found Bruckner's music soul-searching and sublime. Bruckner's music was popularized by the London-based music magazine *Gramophone* (the oldest music magazine in the world, established in 1923 by Compton Mckenzie). His craggy gargantuan symphonies with their resonance and resounding climaxes, rather like giant mountains frozen into music, were ideally suited to the modern era's high fidelity sound.

It is ironical that Bruckner should become a cult figure in London, because he had wanted to settle there when he was jilted by a barmaid. Throughout his life, Bruckner continuously fell in love with young peasant girls, barmaids and waitresses who, without exception, rejected him. Hardly a surprise, for Bruckner was not exactly handsome. In fact, he looked rather like a scarecrow with his close-cropped hair that made him look almost bald, a long crooked nose and a vulture-like neck which made his head wobble. Children laughed and threw stones at him when Bruckner walked the streets of Vienna. In fact, it was not just the girls—life itself seemed to have rejected him from a very early age. He was the eldest of a family of eleven children born in a poor Austrian village. His father died early and Bruckner, who showed musical talent, was loaned to the St. Florian Monastery, which was to be his home more or less throughout his life. His simple faith in God was born there as he learnt to play the organ. As one critic said, not without reason, Bruckner's symphonies are like organ improvisations transcribed for the orchestra. Indeed, throughout his life, Bruckner played the organ with power and beauty, rather like Bach, Buxtehude, and the French composer Cesar Franck. Bruckner, in fact, came to London during the Great Industrial Exhibition, to test, play and promote newly-manufactured organs. Little did he know that one day, all the great orchestras of London would proudly play his symphonies.

Bruckner was always childlike and simple and this innocence can be felt in his music. When he was loaned as a teacher by the St. Florian Monastery to a nearby village school, Bruckner was made to carry human excrement as a daily chore. Bruckner did not protest but carried the buckets full of filth as being part of God's will. The same Bruckner wrote and dedicated his immortal Ninth Symphony to 'Dear God in Heaven'. Bruckner's faith was that they also serve who only stand and wait.

Bruckner is the perfect example of the non-person, the anti-hero, a figure straight out of the novels of Albert Camus and Graham Greene. Like Brahms, he

Anton Bruckner.

never married. But unlike Brahms, he never had a woman like Clara Schumann to help him out. Bruckner wanted to marry, but he always fell in love with women much younger whose answer was an inevitable 'No'! This drove him again and again to mental breakdowns. It seems rather pointless and malicious that some modern critics have tried to link Bruckner with necrophilia. Bruckner would have died of shame.

But the dissection of the Brucknerian mind does not affect his music which is, in one word, glorious. Bruckner's nine symphonies, his Masses and his *Te Deum* are all of a consistently high standard. His symphonies have a direct link with Beethoven. The first movement is a drama of conflict with the soul as the hero, the second movement, usually an adagio, is a song of faith, Bruckner's prayerful communion with God. The third is always a scherzo, a dance of life and the joys of life in nature, and the finale shows the soul triumphing over all opposition. As a man, Bruckner may have been a bit of a clown. But his music is dead serious. A Bruckner symphony is the agonizing cry of a lost soul searching for God in music. To find its equal, we must go back to the chants and prayers of early man.

The Strangled Cry

case of Gustav Mahler (1860-1911) was indeed strange. In music, the van Gogh syndrome does not exist. Everyone knows van Gogh sold only one painting in his lifetime, and became famous only after his death. Bach was forgotten after his death, but during his lifetime, he was reasonably successful. Not so with Mahler. He composed in secret and was famous during his lifetime as a conductor and an artistic director of operas. His symphonies were appreciated by only a handful of his students like Bruno Walter and Otto Klemperer. After his death, Mahler's fame as a composer spread gradually, till the gramophone industry and the LP era made him a cult figure. Indeed Mahler was the van Gogh of music.

Why did Mahler compose in secret? To understand this, you have to appreciate what happened to music in the second half of the 19th century. The world of music at this time was dominated by the spectacle of the opera. On the one hand was Wagner, and on the other, Verdi. It was not the melodic outpouring of Verdi, but of Wagner, from which creative musicians like Mahler and Bruckner drew inspiration. Both accepted the Wagnerian sound universe, but with a difference. They were both composers of the symphony, a musical form that was in urgent need of rejuvenation. So they created the Wagnerian symphony. Said Mahler, in a famous meeting with Sibelius: 'My symphony is the world; it must cover everything, be expansive, gigantic.'

To Mahler, his symphonies may have been the world, but was the world ready for them? Apparently not, as Mahler realized at the premiere of some of his early symphonies. Just as van Gogh was frustrated by the indifference of the art world, Gustav Mahler was physically and mentally demolished by the indifferent, even hostile, reception of his symphonies. Once Mahler realized that success was not to be, he began to compose in secret. His life became divided. Part of it would be lived out as the tyrant of the rostrum, and another would be overtaken by the intense creative artist torn by self-doubt, angst and paranoia, and yet, at a subliminal level, confident of a strange power in him. This confidence made him utter these brave words: 'My time is yet to come,' even after disastrous premieres. Mahler did not merely compose in secret. He felt secretly, very deeply, about things, incidents and personal relationships. Perhaps in no other composer does personal life play such an intimate role in developing creative ideas. In that sense, Mahler was perhaps even more 'romantic' than Wagner or even Liszt. For example, Mahler loved his mother and hated his father. One day, while his parents were having a particularly nasty fight, Mahler, who could not take it any more, rushed out of the house. On the road, he heard the music of a popular hurdy-gurdy. Mahler travelled from the intensely painful to the ridiculous. He later confessed to his wife Alma that this juxtaposition of intensity and levity occurs again and again in his symphonies. He often heard bugles and horns playing across the barracks, a regular childhood experience. His symphonies abound in distant calls of horns, brass and woodwinds, like shadows from the past, making it necessary for Mahler enthusiasts to be acquainted with his life. Donald Mitchell, Alma Mahler and Deryck Cooke have all written evocative books on Mahler.

Mahler's attitude to his Jewishness, towards his wife—young enough to be his daughter—and his obsession with death must be understood by anyone wanting to gain entry into his tension-charged world. Throughout his life, Mahler felt hunted because he was a Jew. He tried to overcome it by converting to Christianity. But it merely added to his angst and loneliness. The tension in his music is the tension of alienation. Because he was obsessed with work, he married late, but felt inadequate and unwanted after marriage. This drove him to the psychiatrist's couch, and a famous meeting with Sigmund Freud. It also broke his health and resulted in premature death. Mahler's music is never far from death. From his childhood, death was his constant companion. He lost his brother and several children. In his Third Symphony, he ushers in the bloom of flowers in an incredible movement, but in another, describes withering flowers symbolizing death. The slow movement of his Fourth Symphony articulates the experience of a walk in a graveyard of children.

Why do all great conductors love Mahler? Why does Mahler appeal to our generation? Mahler makes the strange sensuous world of Wagnerian sound acceptable to us in a symphonic format. Conductors love him because his orchestration is so exciting and unexpected. Take *Nachtmusik* one and two from his Seventh Symphony, or the world-famous *adagietto* from his Fifth Symphony, or the use of a chorus of human voices in the Second and Eighth symphonies. These are some of the most exciting moments in music, and conductors know it. And as far as the modern man is concerned, he finds in Mahler a musical catharsis of all his frustrations.

Chapter 2

Soulitariness

God is Great

The

love for God, the fear of God, and the gratefulness to God has been one of the prime sources of classical music over the centuries. Although the philosopher Nietzsche, an amateur composer, had declared 'God is dead', almost all the major composers have written music that communicates the presence of God in life. Such has been the victory of faith over logic that even a minor composer like John Stainer (1840-1901) has been immortalized by one religious work, *The Crucifixion,* composed in 1887. This composition is performed in England during Christmas as often as Handel's *Messiah.* Rossini, famous for his operas, produced two wonderful religious works—the *Stabat Mater* (1842) and the beautiful *Petite Messe Solennelle* (1863)—both glorious works of the sacred music repertoire. Wagner, who was Nietzsche's friend, was not overtly spiritual. Yet, late in life, he composed *Parsifal,* an opera that is so intensely and ritualistically religious that the listener requires a fair knowledge of the ceremonial aspects of the Roman Catholic religion to appreciate it fully. As a human being, Wagner was mean and nasty; his anti-Jewish feelings are well documented. He was also very unscrupulous in his dealings with people. Yet, he could write a sublime melody like the one given to the clarinet and orchestra in *Parsifal's* 'Good Friday' music.

The contradiction can be resolved if we understand that the central inspiration of Western music has been the song of the soul, expressed through the assertion of the presence of God in life. All the composers from the earliest times till today have done so in traditional forms like the Mass and non-traditional ones like symphonies, quartets and even operas.

The instrument most used to express the discovery of holiness in our lives is the human voice, the oldest known to man. One of the first musical instruments to enter the holy musical circle was the oboe and its earlier versions like the shawm. In the works of Vivaldi, Handel and Bach, the oboe became the voice of the Holy Spirit. Consider Bach's cantata, 'Ich habe genug,' where the bass sings in words that proclaim

Score of Bach's B Minor Mass.

Madrigal singers serenading a lady, an early woodcut illustration.

the composer's innocent faith in God and the oboe creates a garland of silver tones around it.

In the B Minor Mass and the *Christmas Oratorio,* Bach used the oboe to convey the feel of a halo around the head of the Saviour. A unique example of the oboe, the holy instrument, is evident in the First Movement of Beethoven's Fifth Symphony, when suddenly, as the orchestra proclaims the triumph of fate that clutches humanity, the lonely voice of the oboe sounds like a prayer. Given that this symphony was composed soon after the composer discovered his deafness, the passage with the oboe sounds as if the composer was praying for God's mercy.

In the 16th century, songs were in danger of being banned from the church. The church authorities in the famous Council of Trent (1562) were on the verge of banning music altogether from the church, when the composer Palestrina stepped in with a request. He promised to create pure music, appropriate for the church. Thus the historic *Missa Papae Marcelli* was created. It won the case for music and the crisis was averted.

The early sacred music club consists of Palestrina, Orlando de Lassus, Monteverdi, Schutz, Byrd and Tallis. They composed music in specific forms—the Mass, the motet, the cantatas and the madrigal. The last category was marked by the traits of both the sacred and the amorous and was one of the first to start the dichotomy between sacred and non-sacred music, which began as the Renaissance Age passed into the Baroque.

The Baroque masters—Corelli, Bach, Handel and Vivaldi—not only composed religious music in a traditional form but also gave voice to spiritual feelings through instrumental music. In Bach's cantatas, the line between sacred and profane music begins to get blurred and becomes a profound expression of the human soul. In the suites for unaccompanied cello, it was as if Bach prayed through the sublime tones of the cello.

In Handel, the dichotomy is more pronounced. His Italian operas are sensual and amorous, but his late oratorios, *Messiah, Solomon* and *Israel in Egypt* are the cornerstones of music, whose primary aim is to worship God. While Handel, patronized by the English court, lived a sumptuous life, Bach's life was one of austerity, travelling between the Leipzig school and the Leipzig church. He reminds one of the saints in the Old Testament who lived only to obey God's commands. Although Vivaldi was a priest and composed a great deal of sacred music, it is his instrumental concertos that have made him famous. In the last three decades, his religious music was discovered and its incomparable beauty won many admirers. But it is Bach who comes first to mind when we think of this genre.

In Haydn, Mozart and Beethoven, the lines between sacred and secular music almost vanish. Towards the end of his life Haydn composed Masses but his symphonies and string quartets have sublime moments and his most deeply felt religious work, *The Seven Last Words of Christ,* is a series of string quartet movements. Mozart also wrote Masses and other traditional religious music but his operas, like *The Magic Flute,* string quartets and the slow movement of the *Sinfonia Concertante* (K 364) are sublime and spiritually invigorating.

Beethoven's *Missa Solemnis* is a masterpiece in this category, but the conductor Simon Rattle rightly feels that the *Pastoral* Symphony, where Beethoven thanks God for creating this beautiful world, is his most religious work. His last quartets are simply divine.

The Romantics like Liszt, Weber and Mendelssohn wrote traditional religious music but their instrumental music too is deeply heartfelt—silent thoughts rather than entertainment. Neville Cardus wrote of the romantic Bruckner that he did not have to search for God, for he had found Him. Bruckner's symphonies and Masses are like giant stairways to heaven. Chopin, though he did not compose religious music formally, made his own instrument, the piano, sing sublimely in search of the soul. Brahms' *A German Requiem* created a revolution by replacing the standard Latin text. Tchaikovsky's music is a poem on life and death and his *Pathetique* Symphony is like a confession, a profound outpouring of the soul to God.

In the 20th century, composers have favoured traditional religious forms as well as innovative instrumental creations to convey their feelings for God. The glorious beauty of Pergolesi's *Stabat Mater,* composed at the time of Mozart, returns in the *Stabat Mater* of Szymanowski (1926) while the Penderecki *Christmas* Symphony (1979) incorporates the much-loved Christmas carol, 'Silent Night, Holy Night'. Shostakovich, particularly in his Fourteenth Symphony, brings us close to God. Soul-stirring religious works have been composed by the Estonian composer Arvo Pärt while the English composer John Tavener, in his string suite, *The Protecting Veil* (1987), in praise of Virgin Mary, moves us to our very foundations.

As the world continues to oscillate between existential faith and mind-boggling chaos, serious music continues to sing the praise of God.

Go on Gregory

In music the vagaries of fashion are inexplicable. Gregorian Chants have today become immensely popular, outselling most of the music that falls under the ubiquitous term 'classical'. In shops, records of Gregorian Chants which sell under the gimmicky title of 'The Mystery' hardly languish on the shelves. A young art student wanting to start a collection buys the music after listening to an expert. Surprisingly, none of them have been motivated by the fact that Gregorian Chants are now frequently used in TV commercials, which have helped to popularize this form of music. People like the music because they find it sublime, simple and immensely moving.

What are Gregorian Chants? To understand, you have to know a little about a priest called Gregory who lived for 64 years from 540-604. From a priest, he became a Pope and finally a saint. Although ancient tradition makes Gregory one of the most important of all composers, it is doubtful if he was particularly musical. He initially worked with the government, and in his mid-30s, hearing the call of God, he resigned and set about founding monasteries. He was sent by Pope Pelagius II to represent the church and the Holy Roman Empire in Byzantium, where he stayed for seven years. Then Pelagius died of the plague and Gregory was chosen his successor.

His name will be eternally remembered because it is linked with the chants of the Latin liturgy.

This linking did not take place in Gregory's lifetime but some 400 years later. However, in his lifetime, though Gregory did not compose these chants, he supervised and encouraged their collection. He set scholars to sift, codify and legitimize these chants that existed for centuries before him. The collection he supervised was put into a large book called the *Antiphonarium,* which was chained to the altar at St. Peter's in Rome.

But the music couldn't be chained; it spread everywhere: to Switzerland, Germany, France, Spain and England. Gregory could thus claim to be the

Portrait of Pope Gregory.

first universal composer and is today certainly an international name.

What do these songs say? Beautiful thoughts:

> *Peace I leave with you; my peace I give to you, not as the world gives do I give to you/ A new commandment I give to you, that you love one another/ Peace, glory and praise be to the Father and to the Son and to the Holy Ghost/ for ever and ever. Amen.*

What is the structure of these songs? Basically, they are plain songs or songs without any embellishment or decoration, either vocal or instrumental. They are sung prayers.

Unfortunately, in India, one cannot hear Gregorian Chants either in concerts or in churches. That is why appreciation of these wonderful chants will depend on recordings. Record shops all over the country, wherever classical music is sold, do display plenty of recordings of Gregorian Chants.

SPRINGTIME, RINGTIME

'God respects me when I work, but loves me when I sing,' wrote Tagore. In springtime, throughout the history of music, the thoughts of composers have turned to singing, songs and much more.

The most famous of all medieval compositions is the song *Sumer is icumen in,* which entreats the cuckoo to sing loudly. Medieval troubadours and minnesingers sang compulsively about love and the red rose—a habit that remained with composers even in the 19th century. Among two of the most famous songs of spring is one by Grieg (op. 33, no. 2). The music has been arranged for the string orchestra and four-hand piano. Mendelssohn's *Songs Without Words* no. 30 in A is called *Spring*. In England, for a long time, it was nicknamed *Camberwell Green*. This is because Mendelssohn composed it on 1 June 1842, in Camberwell, London.

Arguably, the most famous of all spring music is Vivaldi's *Spring* Concerto from *The Four Seasons*. The concertos are preceded by poems—sonnets which many believe were written by Vivaldi himself. *The Spring* Concerto begins with the lines:

The spring has come and joyfully
Is greeted by the birds with happy song
And the brooks at the breath of zephyr winds
Flow gently murmuring.

The sonnet also makes specific references to 'birdsongs of enchantment' and the 'sleeping goatherd', his 'faithful dog' and the 'pastoral bagpipe with festive sound'. The music describes all these and the happiness it exudes has made it an ever-popular work, which modern research claims as the most suitable music for a car's music-system.

The question of music describing nature or a particular season brings up the controversial issue of programme in music. Is classical music abstract? Can it convey moods and feelings, describe emotions and visuals? While there are many theories, I would like to draw the reader's attention to film music to emphasize the point that there are no golden rules. Mozart's music, such as the Clarinet Concerto, the second movement of the Flute and Harp Concerto, Symphonies nos. 25 and 40, the second movement of Piano Concerto no. 21, and numerous other piano sonatas, trios, string quartets and even religious music, have been used again and again in films. Yet, Mozart's music, experts say, is abstract, and certainly Mozart has never gone on record saying that his music has any objective correlative. Yet all major music directors have used Mozart's compositions in films to enhance the impact of the story and the visuals. Boccherini is another composer of abstract classical forms whose music (the famous minuet) has been used in the film *The Ladykillers* while Beethoven's 'Emperor' Concerto was the theme in *The Lost Weekend*.

Reactions are more precise when the music has a label like Spring. Take Beethoven's violin sonata of the same name, and the *Pastoral Piano* Sonata—both contain music that helps us enjoy the feel of nature. Beethoven published his *Spring* Sonata in 1801. It is in the key of F Major, which is also the key of his *Pastoral* Symphony. It is filled with spontaneous inspiration and contains a little scherzo which is supposed to convey the movement of a squirrel coming in and out of a hole in a tree. This is quite possible because Beethoven was a great observer and has recorded in detail his many walks in the woods. The squirrel episode is a passage of simplicity and innocence, and in total contrast with the Beethoven of the grand symphonies. The *Pastoral Piano* Sonata was published in 1802. In fact it is Beethoven's publisher,

Cranz, who gave it the subtitle which Beethoven knew about, unlike many of his other famous subtitles, like the *Moonlight* Sonata. The entire sonata in four movements is distinctly bucolic in nature, and the season it describes is probably spring, judging by the fact that the composition is in the joyous key of D Major, and by the happy feelings the melodies evoke. Beethoven's own words regarding the *Pastoral* Symphony throw light on the nature of programme music: 'The hearers should be allowed to discover the situation. All painting in instrumental music, if pushed too far, is a failure. The Pastoral Symphony is no picture but something in which the emotions are expressed which are aroused in men by the pleasures of the country.' From this it would seem quite clear that Beethoven sanctioned individual reactions to music. The third movement of this symphony—*Merry Gathering of the Country Folk*—brings to mind paintings depicting springtime.

When Robert Schumann gave the title Spring to his First Symphony in B flat, he used the word with all its symbolic connotations, taking it a step beyond Vivaldi and Beethoven. On 2 September 1840, Schumann succeeded in marrying Clara Wieck after a long and troubled courtship. He composed the *Spring* Symphony to mark the occasion and it is possible that he used the title to suggest the fulfillment of love. In a letter he wrote to the conductor Taubert, he said, 'When you play the symphony, could you breathe into your musicians some feelings of spring? These possessed me when I wrote it. The first trumpet section is intended, as from a height, to invoke an awakening. In the following introduction I wanted to show how everything becomes green; perhaps a butterfly flits past slowly.'

Bruckner's Fourth Symphony is all about love in the medieval world, though it has the title *Romantic* and not *Spring*. Bruckner, a deeply religious man, seldom expressed earthy emotions. This symphony, with its magically haunting horn-calls, is an exception. It breathes the atmosphere of a dense forest with tall trees where a pair of lovers, who have got lost, are calling to each other. It links up with Mahler who, in his symphonies, actually spoke to flowers and meadows. His gigantic Third Symphony has the following movements—*Pan awakes, Summer marches in; What the flowers of the meadow tell me; What the creatures of the forest tell me,* and so on.

Surprisingly, another spring symphony was to be composed in a century tormented by thoughts of nature's death, the destruction of green resulting in ecological imbalance. In 1949, a little more than a hundred years after Schumann, Benjamin Britten wrote his Spring Symphony in which he, ironically, used the text of the medieval poem *Sumer is icumen in*. Indeed the cuckoo sings throughout this work which was inspired, as Britten wrote, 'by a particularly lovely day in East Suffolk'. Britten, inspired by Mahler, wrote a choral symphony in which he used several texts. The one written by Thomas Nashe (1567-1601) gives us good reason to smile even after two World Wars, after experiencing all the hatred, torment, suspicion and greed of modern living. For spring with its smile must come back year after year, and the cycle of seasons must go eternally on:

Spring, the sweet Spring, is the year's pleasant king;
Then bloom each thing, then maids dance in a ring,
Cold doth not sting, the pretty birds do sing,
Cuckoo, jug-jug, pu-we, to-witta-woo!

Requiem

Rest in Peace

may seem surprising, but one of the most popular forms of musical expression with composers of early music to that of the present day has been the requiem or Mass for the dead.

It is important to remember that through this form ('requiem' comes from the Latin term *'requies'* meaning 'to rest'), the composer is not just celebrating a personal involvement but a universal destruction of evil forces. This makes the requiem more than just a poem to death—it becomes an affirmation of eternal life.

A Mass in this form is called a requiem because it begins with the words 'Give them eternal rest, O Lord.' A historical perspective of the requiem Mass is essential for an appreciation of the composers, not because all great composers have written requiems (there are exceptions like Beethoven), but when written as in the case of Mozart, Verdi, Berlioz, Brahms and Fauré, they have become one of their most popular compositions. Statistics taken by the recording industry prove that recordings of requiems are some of their best-selling items.

A requiem Mass is usually divided into eight sections, some of which, like the *Kyrie,* the *Sanctus* and the *Agnus Dei* are common to the regular Mass. But the requiem also adds sections like the *Dies Irae* (Day of Wrath), under which come the *Lacrimosa* and the *Tuba Mirum,* which have evoked some splendid music. What constitutes the eternal appeal of this music? Which composers have given their best in a requiem?

The D Minor *Requiem* (K 626) was Mozart's last composition, and it was left incomplete. As is well known, Mozart died before he could finish the score, and his pupil Franz Sussmayr completed it. In July 1791, Mozart was visited by a mysterious stranger who commissioned him to do a requiem Mass. The secrecy surrounding the commission, and the sinister, tall grey figure with the gaunt serious face (fully exploited in the film *Amadeus*) made a deep impression on the feverish and dying Mozart who saw in the stranger a supernatural warning. Modern research has proved that there is more fiction than fact in this story. The mysterious stranger turned out to be the servant of a Count von Walsegg-Stuppach who intended to claim the work as his own at a memorial service for his wife. All his plans came to nothing because Mozart died before the work could be completed.

The real mystery of the *Requiem,* according to some scholars, is in the fact that although Mozart had left specific instructions with Sussmayr as to how the *Requiem* should be completed, his wife Constanze Mozart came to Sussmayr as a last resort only after all other attempts to complete the *Requiem* had failed. It has been suggested that Mozart's pupil Sussmayr, who was his constant companion in his last years, was actually having an affair with Constanze, and this affair had turned sour by the time Mozart died. Speculations will never cease around Mozart's *Requiem.*

Berlioz's *Requiem,* like Mozart's, is an awe-inspiring work, like Michelangelo's *Last Judgement.* But perhaps the most peaceful, delicate and lyrical of all requiems is the one by the French composer Gabriel Fauré (1846-1924). Fauré was a wonderfully innovative composer, and created some lovely chamber music. But his *Requiem* is something special. It was composed for the soprano, baritone (two of the most cherished roles for singers), chorus, organ and orchestra and is divided into seven movements.

An important point to note is that Fauré omitted the *Dies Irae* section in his *Requiem.* He had a concept of death as being a peaceful, friendly state, and his music is utterly ravishing. Fauré's *Requiem* stands apart from all other requiems as being non-operatic and avoiding the terrors of the Last Judgement.[1] Much of the melodic interest stays in the orchestra, from the soaring string lines in the *Agnus Dei* to the beautiful muted violins in the *Sanctus,* and the unforgettable organ parts delineating Paradise in the movement *In Paradisum.* Fauré, like Gluck before him, makes an attempt to describe the feeling of Paradise in music, and succeeds.

Most requiems follow the Latin text which has come down the centuries, but not the one by Brahms. *Ein Deutsches Requiem,* the famous op. 45 of Brahms, is based on poems in German relating to death. The inspiration for the work came when Brahms' mother died in 1865. Unlike the content of the Mass for the dead, Brahms here addresses all those who mourn, and offers them consolation.

He originally wanted to call it 'A Requiem for Mankind', but later changed the title. This requiem too has some wonderful solos for baritone and soprano, and some of the best singers in the world have sung this great work, which also has some splendid orchestral effects, especially for the timpani. Whether you develop a taste for the more unconventional works of Fauré and Brahms, or the more operatic creations of Verdi, Berlioz and Mozart, appreciation of the requiem is central to an understanding of Western music.

[1] Verdi's *Requiem,* a composition of his last years, is just the opposite–tormented, terrifying and terror-stricken. Although it contains none of Verdi's greatest melodies, it is not a requiem for the weak-hearted. The Duruflé *Requiem,* a modern requiem composed just fifty years ago, is like Fauré's *Requiem,* filled with peace.

Still, Sad Music of Humanity

'April is the cruelest month,' said T.S. Eliot in *The Wasteland*. Somehow in my mind the line is always linked with Easter. What could be more cruel than the image of Christ on the cross? I am reminded of the poem by Edith Sitwell written during the air raids of 1940:

Still falls the rain
Dark as the world of man, black as our loss
Blind as the nineteen hundred and forty nails
Upon the cross...

Creativity—the arts, painting, sculpture, literature and music has turned this barbaric act of nailing a man on a cross into one which can be best described as cathartic. Read Sitwell's poem next Easter as you listen to the two Masses in A flat and E flat by Franz Schubert. This composer is not normally associated with religious music in spite of the fact that he wrote the beautiful *Ave Maria*. But he did write a large number of Masses and the two referred to here are his masterpieces in this genre. The A flat Mass was written in 1822, the year of the *Unfinished* Symphony, and the one in E flat, when he was composing the Quintet in C Major for strings. There is agony, pain and nobility in this music. Somehow the Masses embody for me the essential spirit of Easter.

Schubert's life was unfinished like his famous symphony—the distilled essence of sorrow. It is a feeling you will get in the two Masses. There is tragedy here and yet, a great nobility, like the art of El Greco.

Today we find ourselves in a world of conflict. Let us turn to the Eliot of *Ash Wednesday:*

Suffer us not to mock ourselves with falsehood
Teach us to care and not to care
Teach us to sit still

For stillness and peace in music, I turn to Bach—the Bach of the B Minor Mass, particularly the *Crucifixus* section. I remember the late Theodore Matheisson telling me as the Oxford Mission boys played an instrumental version of this music that Bach saw the angels on a cloud as he wrote it. Matheisson spoke with such sincerity and conviction that you had to believe him. Later, when I heard the original choral version, I realized how right he was. This is music as soft as crushed rose petals, as innocent as a baby's smile. Teach us to sit still it does, but do we listen?

Of all the visual images of Christ's last days on earth, the image of the donkey is to me the most mysterious. We all laugh at the donkey yet that animal had its day in GK Chesterton's poem:

Fools: For I also had my hour
One far fierce hour and sweet
There was a shout about my ears
And palms before my feet...

The donkey for me is the eternal underdog. And when I think of this poem my mind turns to the religious music of Anton Bruckner, music's greatest underdog. Nervous, insecure and bullied by men like Wagner, Bruckner anchored his life on the rock of faith. That was his refuge. His symphonies and Masses are assertions of this faith and make very appropriate music for Easter.

There is one piece of Easter music which through tradition has become associated with Christmas—Handel's *Messiah*. The oratorio for solo voices, choir, harpsichord, organ and orchestra was first performed on 13 April, 1741 in Dublin during Easter. The music dealing specifically with Easter comes in the second part of the oratorio with one of Handel's most beautiful melodies, the contralto song:

He was despised and rejected of men,
man of sorrows and acquainted with grief.

In the same section we have the bass aria: *Why do nations so furiously rage together,* which has a very significant message for us today. The thundering and all-embracing *Hallelujah* chorus comes in the end of part II.

It was in 19th-century England that the Handel masterpiece became linked with Christmas. But Handel composed a complete oratorio about Christ among the shepherds and also His passion, death and resurrection.

Musically, nothing has excited the imagination of composers more than the image of the risen Christ. Handel's *Hallelujah* chorus is perhaps the supreme example. But there are many more. In Beethoven's *Missa Solemnis* there is an awe-inspiring moment when the words of the Mass—*And the third day He rose again according to the scriptures*—burst out. Beethoven here narrates the incident with a device which almost sounds like a thunderclap and brings back memories of the transition between the third and fourth movements of his Fifth Symphony in C Minor. This great moment in the history of civilization has been marvellously depicted in high Baroque art and

Facing pages: An early organ book illustration. Below: Early chorus singers from England.

equally brilliantly by Gustav Mahler, not only in his *Resurrection* Symphony but also in his *Symphony of a Thousand* which is heaven-storming. There is a bit of Raphael and Rubens in Mahler and his music is best appreciated through a comparison with paintings. I remember the Third Symphony being packaged in the golden years of the LP with paintings by Gustav Klimt. My imagination was stoked by all the flowers and Klimt's habit of using gold.

I am often asked about the appropriateness of music for an occasion. Apart from music that is obviously written with a religious context—Masses, the *Stabat Mater,* the *Miserere,* the *Dixit Dominus,* the *Gloria,* the *Ave Verum Corpus* (one of Mozart's greatest works) and the *Ave Maria,* there is quite a lot of music that may not have an overt religious context but is deeply spiritual. A more contemporary example compared to Mahler is Henryk Gorecki's Symphony no. 3, subtitled 'Symphony of Sorrowful Songs'. It has three tranquil movements based on poems written about Hitler's attack on Poland in 1939:

Where has he gone
My dearest son?
Perhaps during the uprising
The cruel enemy killed him.
Tell me, why did you kill my son?

One way of answering this eternal question is to think of the closing pages of the great Masses from Monteverdi to Mozart, Beethoven to Berlioz—the *Dona nobis pacem* (Grant us peace). Eliot would have said, *'Shanti, Shanti, Shanti.'* But for me the greatest moment of *Shanti* comes in the *Et incarnatus est* passage from Schubert's Mass in E flat. It brings to my mind thoughts that are too deep for tears.

Formulations

Simply About Symphonies

The most important form in classical music is perhaps the symphony. It is also the most misused word in the English language. I have heard people talking about a symphonic sunset, and also a symphonic omlette. We must have a clear notion of what a symphony is, so that the ambiguity of its usage does not confuse us musically.

A symphony is a large-scale musical work in four movements or sections. Although symphonies have been written for solo instruments—the piano for instance—we should think of the orchestra when we think of the symphony. The epithet 'large-scale' needs to be clarified. The concept of what constitutes 'largeness' varies from composer to composer. For instance, the whole of a Mozart symphony would fit into just the first movement of Beethoven's *Eroica* Symphony.

The Beethoven Age followed shortly after Mozart, so you can imagine what happened to the symphony in the hands of late romantic composers like Bruckner and Mahler. The symphony has simply grown larger and larger. Mozart's most ambitious symphonies last no longer than 25 minutes while Mahler's Ninth Symphony lasts nearly 90 minutes. But interestingly, as we come close to the 20th century, we find symphonies getting shorter and shorter, as in the symphonies of Sibelius, Prokofiev and Stravinsky. But classical precision was also shown by French composers like Georges Bizet in the mid-19th century.

Although there are exceptions like Schubert's *Unfinished* Symphony (with two movements), and Mozart's *Prague* Symphony (with three movements), the majority of symphonies are in four movements, though there are some like Beethoven's *Pastoral* Symphony which have more. A symphony is actually a piece of musical architecture, a house with four rooms. The house has a portico which is the introduction of the symphony. Now, this introduction is most varied in Haydn who was the father of the symphony. Usually the introduction is a slow, solemn movement as in Haydn's *Clock* and *London* symphonies, Mozart's

Beethoven conducting the Ninth Symphony (anonymous).

Symphony no. 39, and Beethoven's Seventh Symphony. But it can also be different. My vote for the most unique symphonic introduction goes to Haydn's Symphony no. 103 which begins with a solo roll of drums, and is appropriately nicknamed 'Drum Roll'.

The introduction prepares you for the first movement or the first room of our symphonic house. Here the music is usually fast-paced, though there are exceptions like Shostakovich's Symphony no. 6 which begins with a solemn, slow movement. The first movement has two themes or melodies, and they interact to form a third theme which brings the movement to a close.

The second room in the house is one for meditation and reverie. It is the slow movement, and is very lyrical and sweet. Some of the greatest music in the world is in the slow movements of symphonies, though in some symphonies like Beethoven's *Choral,* the slow movement is placed elsewhere in the work. As you get familiar with the symphonies, you'll have your special favourite slow movements, but highly recommended are those of Beethoven's Fourth, Seventh and Ninth Symphonies, Mozart's *Jupiter,* Haydn's no. 88, Brahms' no. 4 and Bruckner's no. 7, to mention just a few from the treasure house.

The third room is the room for dancing, variously known as the minuet or the scherzo, depending on the speed of the music. This dance music is usually played by the full orchestra, and also by a small group of instruments. When played by a smaller group, it is called a 'trio'.

The most gorgeous third movements are the ones in Mozart's Symphony no. 39, Schubert's *The Great Symphony,* Bruckner's *Romantic* and Tchaikovsky's brilliant *Pathetique.*

The symphony ends in a blaze of glory in the fourth movement. It is a triumph of faith and an affirmation of hope, the most typical example being the fourth movement of Beethoven's Fifth Symphony, whose majestic close is equivalent to a catharsis. Brahms' First Symphony also ends on a tremendous note of triumph. But there are exceptions like Tchaikovsky's *Pathetique* Symphony, which ends not with a bang but a fading whisper.

But begin with Haydn, Mozart and Beethoven, then move on to Schubert, Schumann, Mendelssohn, Dvorak, Bruckner, Mahler, Sibelius and Tchaikovsky. There is no mistaking the power and the glory of the symphony. It is one of the greatest achievements of mankind.

Contrast+Contest= Concerto

Youngsters often ask me: 'Which is the best way to start a friendship with the world of Bach, Beethoven and Mozart?' My answer is: 'Cultivate the concerto.' In 1952, Ralph Hill wrote in his famous book *The Concerto,* 'In recent days a vast army of music lovers has discovered the concerto. Each generation has to make its own discoveries, and discovery is ever-new though the art-form of music may be old.' He attributed the easy approachability of the concerto to the fact that it 'spells dazzle, display, delight, dexterity, that it is spotlighting a performer and the instrument, an impressive example of mental concentration and physical endurance, an exciting contest between a solitary artist and a full orchestra with victory on the side of the soloist.'

In fact, one of the best ways to listen to a concerto is to think of the entire musical form as a symbol of the struggle between an individual and society and the beautiful musical dialogue established between the two. The greatest example of this is the slow movement of Beethoven's Fourth Piano Concerto. Beethoven took the idea from Gluck's opera *Orfeo ed Euridice,* in which Orpheus plays the lyre to tame the raging Furies. In Beethoven's concerto the Furies are represented by the full orchestra, in an angry outburst. When the solo enters, it is at first timid. But gradually the sound of the piano gets louder and louder and the orchestra becomes more and more subdued. At the close of the movement, the orchestra has been tamed by the soloist, and they make music together in harmony. As Ralph Hill puts it, 'The effort of the soloist and orchestra is not a combat but a carefully planned cooperation which has its objective—the provision of contrast in tone-amount and tone colour. In sober terms a concerto is a musical composition intended to display the capacities of a musical instrument through the skill and artistry of the performer.' But the view that a concerto is a kind of symphony composed for a Horowitz, a Heifetz or a Menuhin is a very limited one. The presence of a brilliant instrumentalist may inspire a composer but the music transcends mere dazzle and dexterity. For example, Mozart wrote his Horn Concertos for the horn player Ignaz Leutgeb and the Clarinet Concerto for Anton Stadler.

The concertos of Walton and Shostakovich were originally written for Heifetz and Oistrakh. They are performed by violinists who see in the music a universal beauty that goes beyond the individual. The violin concertos by Walton, Korngold, Sibelius and Shostakovich flow like a peaceful river circling a volcano. The music erupts and then becomes serene, tranquil and meditative. It is like alternating between calm and chaos. The basic appeal of the concerto is in its variety. It is youthful music, full of spring and freshness. I recommend the concerto to beginners because a concerto has all the elements of classical forms. In the cadenzas or display sections, it is like a solo recital. It has the essence of the symphony as played out by the orchestra and chamber music in highlighting individual instruments.

The earliest concertos were vocal and not instrumental. The most famous of these is Mozart's *Exsultate Jubilate,* which though called a motet is actually a concerto in the usual three movements. The first movement is a tumultuous jubilation, the second is a meditation and the last a glorious *Hallelujah.* It conforms to the solo concerto, except that the soloist is a soprano.

In the Baroque Age, the concerto grosso, meaning a contrast between different groups of the orchestra, was popular. The most famous examples of this form are the six *Brandenburg* Concertos by Bach. These feature a wide variety of soloists—oboe, flute, horn, trumpet, etc. The effect is like a sonic carpet filled with the most magical patterns of sound. No single instrument predominates. There are concertos where wind instruments are used and there are those like the Third and the Sixth for strings. Handel is the master of the concerto grosso for strings. His 12 concerto grossi for strings (op. 6) are masterpieces in this genre and I would recommend the one in D Major (op. 6, no. 5) for its grand evocation of the Baroque world. It's like visiting a magnificent cathedral. For modern versions you could try Bartok's *Concerto for Orchestra.* This work is in five movements and alternates between the fast and the slow, establishing a dialogue between the orchestra and various instruments. This is a modern interpretation of the kind of concertos Bach wrote in the *Brandenburg* set. British composers like Ralph Vaughan Williams, Benjami Britten and Michael Tippett have revived the kind of string concertos that Handel wrote.

Mozart was the king of solo concertos. You could spend a lifetime listening to and loving Mozart's concertos for the piano, horn, clarinet, bassoon, violin and flute. I particularly love the piano concertos, which can now be enjoyed on original instruments and on the modern piano. My favourite violin concerto is the Third and I love the Clarinet Concerto. The four horn concertos have been my friends since I was in college.

Fragment of a violin concerto in C Major composed by Beethoven in 1792.

Don't miss Haydn's Trumpet Concerto and his piano and cello concertos. Beethoven took the concerto form beyond Haydn and Mozart in writing one great violin concerto, five piano concertos and a wonderful triple concerto. The romantics added dazzle, virtuosity and a special kind of dream to the concerto. This includes the Cello Concerto of Schumann, the Mendelssohn Violin Concerto and the piano concertos of Chopin and Liszt. Composers like Dvorak in his violin and cello concertos, Tchaikovsky and Sibelius in their violin and piano concertos, gave the form vivid life. As Ralph Hill put it, 'The modern concerto is rooted in the classical concerto. It differs from those composed during the classical and romantic periods in its spirit and musical content; it follows the trend of all creative music in that it seeks not only to reflect moods and emotions but to express thoughts and philosophy.' In this category I would include the concertos of Prokofiev, Elgar and Shostakovich and the violin concerto of Alban Berg, a mysterious work composed for Alma Mahler's daughter.

Which then are the popular solo instruments used in a concerto? In the case of the concerto grosso, there are no restrictions. Bartok, in his *Concerto for Orchestra,* uses a wide range. The solo concertos feature the piano, violin, cello (the most popular), flute, oboe, horn and trumpet. Mozart, Weber and Spohr wrote wonderful concertos for the clarinet and there are quite a few for the trombone. Walton wrote a concerto for the tuba. There are wonderful concertos for the harp, guitar, mandolin and organ. In fact, the concerto covers the entire tone colour of the orchestral universe, highlighting the one that catches the composer's fancy. The presence of a virtuoso player, of course, acts as a source of inspiration. Vivaldi and Mozart wrote concertos for an array of exotic instruments for particular players.

Of all the concerto composers after Mozart and Beethoven, the one I cherish most is Johannes Brahms. He belongs to no category but himself and his two piano concertos, the glorious violin concerto and the double concerto for violin and cello, should be an essential part of the listening programme of all classical enthusiasts. The soft, mysterious beginning of the Second Piano Concerto, its tranquil slow movement with the accent on the cello, the stormy beginning of the First Piano Concerto, and the slow movements of the Violin Concerto and the Double Concerto have brought joy and happiness to my life.

Allegro con brio
Flauto
Con Oboi
Due Oboe
Con Basso
Due Fagotti
Due Corni
Due Violini
Due Viole
Basso
Violino Principale

Transcribe, Transform, Transfigurate

One of the most popular and important forms of composition involving composers from Handel to Shostakovich through four centuries are transcriptions.

Transcriptions are basically a re-arrangement of music: symphonies, operas and songs for a band, the piano, cello, an ensemble or any other instrument that finds a good and enterprising exponent. Suppose you are a double-bass player or a cellist and need to widen your repertoire. You will take a work, say by Mozart or Beethoven, and arrange it for your instrument. A cellist who does this very frequently is Mischa Maisky and he has transcribed music by Bach, Handel, Gluck and Lully for cello and piano or even cello and orchestra. Maisky has transcribed Luigi Boccherini's famous *Minuet,* originally in the form of a string quintet, for the cello and piano combination, and Schubert's *Moment Musical* no. 3 in F Minor, originally for the piano but transcribed for the cello.

The great conductor and transcriber Leopold Stokowski has also transcribed the same *Moment Musical* for the orchestra to stunning effect. Richard Strauss had a more romantic alternative to the term transcription and called it 'transfiguration'. The more prosaic term is arrangement. When a composer uses material from his earlier work in a later opus, that's a parody. Often Bach used a theme from an earlier work in a later cantata. So did Handel. For instance, the song 'O Death, where is thy sting? O Grave, where is thy victory?' from the late work *Messiah,* is a parody of an earlier soprano and counter tenor duet from Handel's Italian period. Composers also transcribed their works for two-hand piano to popularize the original, especially in the Romantic Age.

A very special form of transcription, *Harmoniemusik*, music for a small wind band, was in vogue in the last quarter of the 18th and the first quarter of the 19th centuries. Haydn, Mozart and Beethoven composed for the medium. The aristocrats and nobility wanted music in the background while eating and drinking. *Harmoniemusik* was so popular during Mozart's days

Copper engraving of Mozart.

that he used a theme from the earlier opera *The Marriage of Figaro* and put it in the banquet scene of *Don Giovanni.* The composer Joseph Triebensee arranged for the wind band the most attractive songs and melodies from Mozart's operas—*Don Giovanni, The Marriage of Figaro, The Magic Flute* and *The Abduction from the Seraglio.* Today ensembles like the Linos and the Europa Symphony and others play and record these transcriptions and they make delightful listening. Your favourite songs come alive on the oboes, bassoons and a combination of the most sonorous wind instruments.

Transcriptions are basically a way of spreading the magic of the music. The conductor Leopold Stokowski, in the famous film *Fantasia,* arranged Bach's *Toccata and Fugue in D Minor* for the orchestra. This was in the early 1940s and Stokowski's transcriptions of Bach and other composers contributed immensely to the spread of classical music.

Franz Liszt was the king of transcribers. He transcribed just about everything for the piano, just as Maisky does today for the cello. Liszt wanted to have a wide repertoire and make his regular concerts more entertaining. Joseph Triebensee and Johann Wendt had popularized operas through their arrangements for wind bands. Now Liszt arranged operas for the piano. His arrangement for *Don Giovanni* was not merely the popular tunes in another form—it was a fantasy on the piano based on Mozart's themes. Liszt called it *Reminiscences de Don Juan* and his touch made it sound almost like an original work. He did something similar with other operas—Verdi's *Rigoletto* whose transcription he called a 'paraphrase', Donizetti's *Lucia di Lammermoor,* Tchaikovsky's *Eugene Onegin* and, of course, operas by Rossini and Wagner. A transcriber of unusual sensitivity, Liszt helped popularize Beethoven's symphonies at a time when the original works were seldom performed. Liszt's arrangements of the Fifth Symphony and the *Pastoral* for the piano are wonderful creations and form part of the repertoire of many pianists today. But he was perhaps most creative and original in his transcription of Schubert's songs. As the critic Bryce Morrison says, 'Liszt considered Schubert the most poetic of all composers and his transcriptions of no less than 56 of Schubert's songs form an eloquent tribute of one genius to another. Lying somewhere between free paraphrase and simple replica, they remain uncannily faithful to the freshness and innocence of the originals whilst adding an extra dimension of idiosyncrasy and sophistication.'

These words wonderfully summarize the quality and spirit of a good transcription as the ones created by the composer Arnold Schoenberg of the symphonies of Mahler and Bruckner. In 1918, Schoenberg joined Alban Berg and Anton Webern to form the *Association for Private Musical Performances.* As Alban Berg put it, 'Schoenberg's main aim was the adequate presentation of music, contemporary and otherwise, which had not been given the attention it deserved on account of prejudice and poor performance.' Mahler's symphonies were totally ignored during his lifetime. Schoenberg's association, with the help of Hanns Eisler, Erwin Stein and Karl Rankl transcribed Mahler's Fourth, Sixth and Seventh Symphonies and Bruckner's Seventh Symphony. The instruments used were the early ones—horn, violin, viola, cello, double bass, piano and harmonium. These ensemble arrangements are considered landmark achievements and have earned the two composers a place in history.

It's interesting to have a composer arrange one of his compositions for a different combination. One of Mozart's flute concertos has an oboe version and Beethoven arranged his Violin Concerto for the piano. Brahms did this often, the most representative examples being his clarinet and viola sonatas.

Behind the transcription there is always an instrumentalist, a small ensemble or a quartet group who request the composer to specially compose for the instruments they play. From Joseph Triebensee to Franz Liszt, Franz Liszt to Arnold Schoenberg and now Mischa Maisky, transcriptions have kept music alive from generation to generation, often making an evangelical contribution to the resurrection and future status of the composer which was the philosophy behind the transcriptions of Liszt and Schoenberg.

The Charmed Chamber

of the most pleasurable ways of entering the world of classical music is to listen to chamber compositions. The word 'chamber' says it all. It is music that can be played inside a chamber or a room as opposed to the concert hall. A lot of music in this category is played in concerts, and in some musically vibrant cities like London, there are special halls for chamber music. Chamber also implies a small group of instruments, strictly two to nine in number, exceeding which it becomes an orchestra. Chamber music is otherwise called 'music for friends'.

Almost all the great composers have played chamber music. Haydn and Mozart played chamber music together, so did Schubert with his friends. Certain composers were great chamber music creators, like Bach and Handel, Haydn and Mozart, Beethoven and Schubert and I should also mention Brahms whose most profound music is probably in his quartets, quintets and trios. Mendelssohn, Schumann and Dvorak also composed some wonderful chamber works, and in the modern age there has been Shostakovich. Composers like Rossini, Verdi, Wagner, Mahler and Bruckner are not known for their chamber music but even they, manipulators of big forces, attempted to compose small, intimate works. Bruckner composed a quintet which is often recorded and makes for good listening. Verdi composed a string quartet, which is attractive. Wagner's *Siegfried Idyll* is chamber-like in mood. Mahler played chamber music but, unlike Bruckner, has left no authentic chamber works.

To feel the pulse of true chamber music, you must listen to Haydn, Mozart, Beethoven, Schubert and Brahms, whom I call the 'Big Five' of chamber music. Amongst the different categories of this music, it is the piano trio that intrigues me the most. It is the holy trinity of music—the triumphant triad—and has brought out some of the best from the great composers. The piano trio originated in the duo sonata, that is, compositions for violin or cello, played with a keyboard accompaniment. Composers like Stamitz, Pleyel, Carl

Score of Haydn's String Quartet.

Philipp Emanuel Bach and his brother Johann Christian Bach wrote a lot of works for this form. Sometimes these duo sonatas used to be accompanied by a third instrument, a cello or a viola da gamba, which was a drone instrument. Three was not a crowd, for slowly, as in the hands of Haydn, an integrated triad was formed. Haydn and Mozart wrote the first real piano trios. Bach's son, C.P.E. Bach, for instance, said that his sonatas could be played by any one of the instruments: violin, cello or even the keyboard. Obviously, the form had not become integrated until Haydn emerged. Haydn composed some 40 piano trios and during his lifetime many of his symphonies were also turned into piano trios to popularize the compositions. Haydn's piano trios are really compositions for three instruments—piano, violin and cello—each having a special role. Even if you can't listen to all 40, try out the *Gypsy* Trio with the *Hungarian* Rondo. It is his most famous trio and because of the nickname has become more popular than the others. But they all make delightful listening and have been served well by recordings. Unlike Haydn who wrote piano trios throughout his life, which is why Schumann found them of no special importance, Mozart reserved his most mature years for the form. Mozart's four great piano trios are the E Major (K 542), the E flat (K 502), the G Major (K 564) and the C Major (K 548). They contain the best of Mozart, and in the G Major Trio he uses the famous melody, 'Three blind mice, see how they run'—which must have been based on a folk tune. Apart from the piano trios Mozart also wrote a clarinet trio which was scored for the piano, the clarinet, and his favourite instrument, the viola. But perhaps Mozart's greatest trio composition is his divertimento for string trio, which was also a very late work. It was scored for the violin, viola and cello and can be considered one of the most glorious masterworks of chamber music.

Beethoven made the piano trio his very own, and contributed three outstanding works. Of the two op. 70 compositions, the first, nicknamed *Ghost,* is marked by a haunting slow movement, one of Beethoven's greatest creations. In the *Archduke* Trio (op. 97), a great work in every sense of the term, all the four movements are brilliant. The slow movement ranks with the most profound music Beethoven created. Schubert wrote two fascinating piano trios in B flat and E flat. The B flat trio's opening movement gave birth to a very popular song of the forties: 'When you are in love,' also known as 'Over the waves'. Like all Schubert's music, the piano trios are filled with wonderful melodies. Schumann wrote three piano trios and Mendelssohn one, a masterwork. But the greatest piano trio composer after Beethoven is probably Brahms. I would strongly recommend you listen to his Piano Trio no. 1 (op. 8), which he revised late in life. It is the quintessence of melancholy. Dvorak's *Dumky* Trio is justifiably famous. It is more like a divertimento and its six movements are tinged with the sadness of the *dumka*.

To understand what has happened to the piano trio in the modern age, we must turn to the two piano trios of Shostakovich. The first is a one-movement work and is remarkable for being the composition of a 16-year-old student. It is a very romantic work which often reminds one of Rachmaninoff. The second trio

Archduke Rudly. Beethoven dedicated the piano trio op. 97 known as Archduke *to him.*

was written in 1944 and is a lament for the human lives lost in World War II. It is a tribute to Mahler, a composer Shostakovich adored. The piano trio has brought together some of the greatest instrumentalists of the modern age. Pianists like Rudolf Serkin, Artur Schnabel, Wilhelm Kempff and Daniel Barenboim have played piano trios. So have cellists like Pablo Casals, Pierre Fournier and Jacqueline du Pré, as also some of the top violinists like Jascha Heifetz, who played trios regularly. There are, in fact, two ways in which trios are interpreted. In some areas, great instrumentalists like Schnabel or Heifetz form groups and in others there are piano trio groups who specialize in playing them. The piano, the violin and the cello, when played together, make a triumphant triad and have brought to life some of the best music from the composers.

The Soul of Music

sonata evolved over a period of 125 years from Scarlatti to Beethoven, during which time it rose to total supremacy as a musical structure. The word 'sonata' simply means a 'sound piece' as opposed to cantata, a 'sung piece'. In other words, the sonata is primarily an instrumental composition.

In the early 17th century, the term 'sonata' was applied to a musical composition in several clearly defined sections having varying speed. In this form it was close to the suite or the partita—terms used for a garland of dance movements at the time of Bach and Couperin. The sonata evolved in the hands of composers like C.P.E. Bach, Haydn and Mozart into a three or four-movement form clearly distinguished from the suite. As the term became widely accepted, a division between the secular and the sacred became apparent.

The *sonate da chiesa* or church sonata contained music of lofty tone, and the *sonata da camera* or chamber sonata tended to become more dance-like. These complex terms were soon dropped by composers who simply thought of sonatas as lightweight or highly serious. From Scarlatti to Mozart, Beethoven to Brahms, sonatas have been composed for a wide combination of instruments—for piano and other instruments ranging from the flute to the trombone and all the members of the string family. There have been sonatas for solo cello, solo violin, string orchestra and even sometimes for voice and piano. But the most important sonatas have been composed for the solo piano, for the cello and piano and for the violin and piano.

The cello sonata is comparatively rare. There are the ravishing sonatas of Bach and Vivaldi. Bach originally composed these for the viola da gamba but they are also played and recorded today on the modern cello. Apart from these two Baroque giants, Luigi Boccherini composed some cello sonatas, but for the next great cello sonatas we must stop at the door of Beethoven. He wrote them during the three periods of his life—early, middle and late—and they contain some of his

HARMONY
IMMORTALITY
MELODY
Sonatas
for the Pianoforte
by
L. van Beethoven.
Edited by E. PAUER.
LONDON, AUGENER & Co.
WEST-END BRANCH
BRIGHTON BRANCH

Facing page: Illustration of the decorative opening page of an early edition of Beethoven's Piano Sonata.
Below: Autographed page of Beethoven's Piano Sonata Appasionata.

The opening bars of Purcell's well-known Golden *Sonata.*

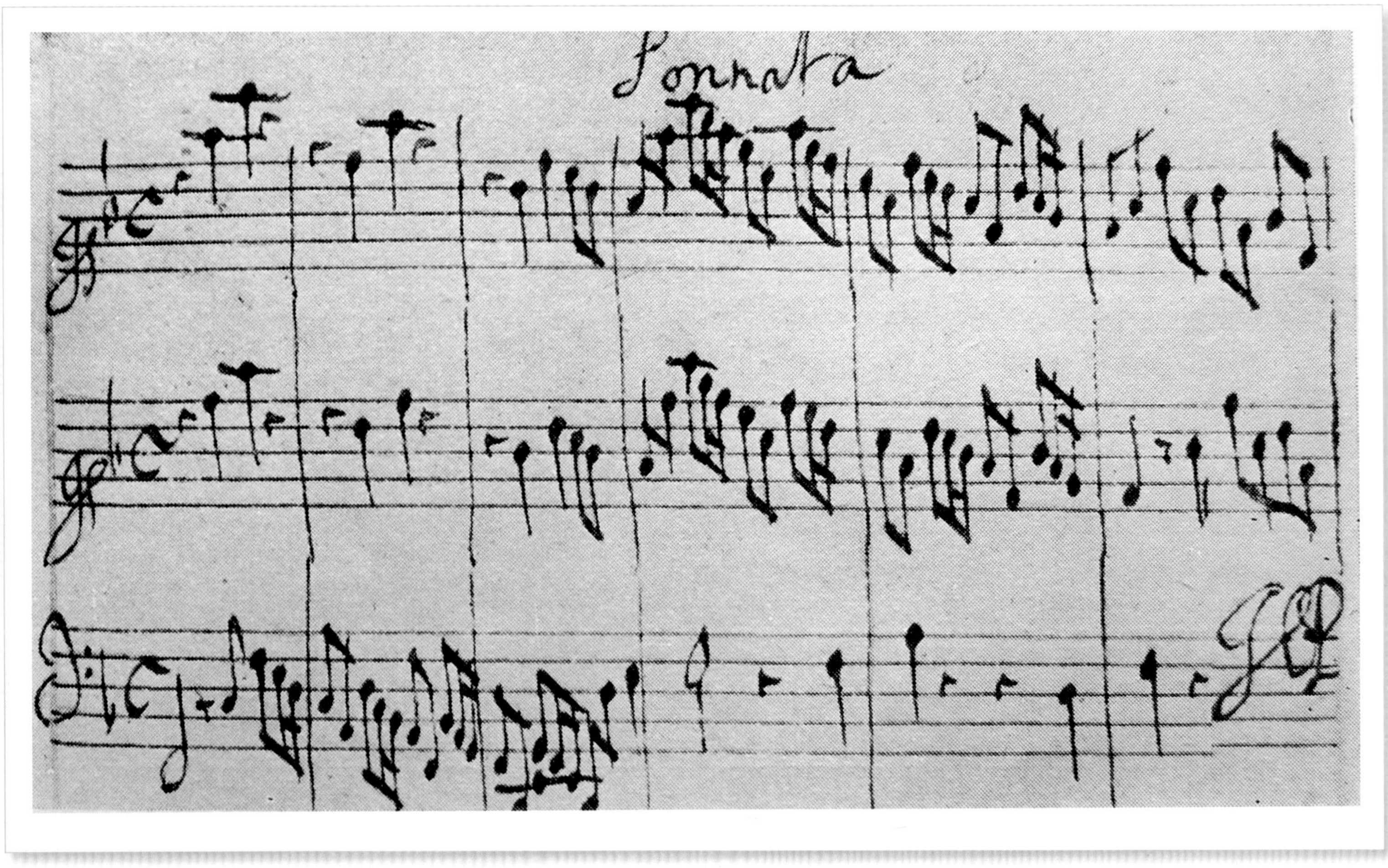

most intimate and poignant music. After Beethoven, some wonderful cello sonatas have been composed by Mendelssohn and Brahms. Chopin also composed a cello sonata, and closer to our century there have been works by Claude Debussy and Shostakovich.

Violin sonatas were far more ubiquitous and have been the heart and soul of major composers. If you want to sample the best in violin sonatas move from Bach and Vivaldi to Mozart. That great master wrote some of his most beautiful music in the violin sonata format. Beethoven wrote some tremendous works, including the famous *Spring* and *Kreutzer* sonatas. Schubert ravishes us with his delightful inventions. Weber's violin sonatas are joyous. But after Beethoven, the greatest violin sonatas have been written by Brahms (three), Cesar Frank and Edvard Grieg, and they are justifiably often performed in the concert hall.

But the heart of the sonata structure is the unique storehouse for solo piano left behind by composers from Mozart to Prokofiev. Modern composers fight shy of using the term 'sonata' for their solo piano compositions. They use phrases like 'Cosmos 3', 'Metamorphosis 1' or 'Octogram'. They probably feel that so much beautiful music has been written for the solo piano in the sonata form that nothing more can be said on the subject.

The piano sonata really began with Domenico Scarlatti. A great majority of the compositions which he called sonatas are in single movements very often limited to one rhythmic or melodic idea. But some of his sonatas do have an element of contrast, which is the most important aspect of the sonata. It was Bach's son, C.P.E. Bach, and later Haydn and Mozart who settled the form of the piano sonata as having an opening movement of great dramatic power, followed by a slow movement of meditative beauty, and finally a climax in a dance-like form called rondo.

Mozart produced about 20 sonatas but it is with the 32 piano sonatas of Beethoven that the sonata, if we may use a cricket metaphor, scored a 'double century'. Beethoven enlarged the scope of the sonata in every way. He made the first movement as in pieces like the *Waldstein,* the *Appassionata* and the *Hammerklavier* into a drama of Shakespearean proportions with the catharsis worked out in the final movement. His slow movements became a document of the soul as in his op. 10, no. 3. As the sonatas flowed, Beethoven's music became more profound in the slow movements until we reach the masterpieces of his last period[1].

Beethoven called the dance movement scherzo—a violent storm of emotions—culminating everything into a brilliant finale. Schubert wrote some 15 sonatas and they are more lyrical and intimate, and a class apart. Brahms wrote three, of which the third is a work of tremendous grandeur seldom performed because of its difficulties. Closer to our time Alexander Scriabin, Rachmaninoff, Paul Hindemith and Sergei Prokofiev have all written piano sonatas.

The romantics thought it wise to call solo piano music by other names and they invented titles like ballade, caprice, rhapsody, intermezzo, scherzo, fantasy and night pieces or nocturnes. Truly, the sonata has become a legend.

[1] See The Great Testament, p. 23.

The Heart of the Matter

The string quartet is the purest, the most personal and intimate of musical forms. Ever since it was created by Joseph Haydn, composers have turned to this sound world of two violins, a viola and a cello, to express the thoughts closest to their hearts. When Mozart wanted to say in music all the feelings of friendship for a fellow composer he chose the string quartet (the set known as Haydn Quartets). When Beethoven wanted to express his thanks to the Almighty for recovering from a grave illness he turned to the string quartet (no. 15 in a minor op. 132). Many centuries later when the composer Leos Janacek sought a musical expression for very personal love letters he selected the string quartet (no. 2, *Intimate Letters*). Shostakovich chose to express his closeness to death and his hatred of war through this medium (quartet no. 8 and no. 14). The composer Bela Bartok, one of the great masters of the 20th century expressed his reactions of living in a stress filled traumatized world through a series of string quartets, a set of six which most serious musicians feel are the greatest in this form after Beethoven, though, I would also include the greatest of the Shostakovich string quartets as being on a par with the Bartok set.

Through the centuries this pure classical medium, the very heart of serious music, has not altered its structure. Other forms like the symphony, the sonata has been altered by the romantics and the moderns. But formally the string quartet remains the song of the four major string instruments (two violins, one viola and one cello) since the days of Haydn. Yes, some composers close to our times like Shostakovich has added more than the original four movements planned by Haydn or even condensed them all to one movement but the essential spirit of the medium has not altered, its purity, simplicity and sublimity has been accepted by all composers. Take the case of Verdi. Essentially an opera composer he turned to chamber music towards the end of his life. What medium did he choose? The string quartet of course. In other words, the string quartet is the quintessential chamber music format. And the reason why the composers from the classical age to the modern have loved it is because the form is actually a symphony in microcosm. Haydn, the inventor of the form, we know was a symphony specialist. In the string quartet he created what can be termed a symphony in miniature having four movements that followed the structure of the symphony, but which was playable by a group of friends in a room. The range of moods expressed by the string quartet is akin to the spectrum of feelings expressed by the symphony, it roars, it weeps, it dances and it affirms and celebrates.

Which are the great string quartets? Let us start with Haydn. There is the *Lark* Quartet (op. 64, no. 5), the *Emperor* (op. 76, no. 3) and *Sunrise* (op. 76, no. 4). Mozart's *Haydn* Quartets are his most brilliant works in this genre. They are (G Major KV 387, D Minor KV 421, E flat KV 428, B flat KV 458, A Major KV 464 and C Major KV 465). Although I have singled out a few from Haydn and Mozart they wrote a great deal more in this form and they are all of the highest quality. In the case of Beethoven I would recommend the three op. 59 quartets know as *Rasoumovsky,* op. 74 *Harp* called thus because of the use of pizzicato strings and the five last quartets E flat op. 127, B flat op. 130, C sharp Minor op. 131, which the composers considered his greatest work in this genre, A Minor op. 132, which I have already mentioned and last quartet in F Major op. 135. Afther Beethoven, I suggest you concentrate on the quartets of Schubert, Dvork, Janacek, Tchaikovsky, Shostakovich and Bartok.

The recording industry has always favoured the string quartet and there have been great quartet groups who have played and recorded the masterpieces in this medium. *The Busch* Quartet, *The Hungarian* Quartet, *The Amadeus* Quartet, *The Beethoven* Quartet, *The Alban Berg* Quartet are a few of the groups who have recorded string quartets from Haydn to the outstanding Shostakovich.

The magic of four instruments have fascinated composers. By taking out the second fiddle and replacing it with instruments like the piano, flute, guitar, oboe and bassoon composers have created different patterns of sound while retaining the format of four. The most popular of these combinations has been the piano quartet and Mozart, Schumann, Dvorak and Faure have written wonderful works in this form. Bach's flute quartets and the guitar quartets of Boccherini are exquisite. Mozart wrote a wonderful oboe quartet.

Throughout the history of music after the classical age of Haydn and Mozart, the concept of chamber music for the composers has been dominated by the string quartet. Every composer has respected it as being the heart of the matter. And rightly so judging by the sheer quality of music, for the composers have poured their heart and soul into this format.

A string quartet group. Violinist and composer Henri Vieuxtemps as the first voilinist.

PASTORAL PANEGYRIC

The word 'pastoral' is one of the most intriguing in the world of arts. It is often equated with landscape painting in music, but as a concept, is a lot more than that. A pastoral is actually a landscape of the mind and of love which is a combination of the divine and the human. Its roots can be traced to the Bible. In a way, David as a shepherd boy, who killed the giant Goliath with a stone, was the first pastor and his psalms[1] have often been set to music to communicate the ambivalence of the concept:

I will praise Thee O Lord with my whole heart
I will show forth all Thy marvellous works.

The 'marvellous works' are, of course the nature, the sky, the sun, thunder, lightning, the trees, the birds, and all that comprises the natural world.

This is what the creators of pastoral music—Beethoven, Vivaldi, Handel, Dvorak, Mahler, Vaughan Williams—and painters like Giorgione, Jean Baptiste Camille Corot, Francois Boucher and William Holman Hunt celebrate. Indeed Giorgione's painting *The Tempest* may have been seen by Beethoven for it comes to mind in the famous approach of the storm in the Sixth Symphony. One of the most emotional expositions of the concept is provided by the poet Robert Browning in the poem *Two in the Campagna:*

The champaign with its endless fleece
Of feathery grasses everywhere!
Silence and passion, joy and peace,
An everlasting wash of air...

[1] David, the shepherd boy, was also a musician who played the harp and when he became king, composed the Psalms, known as the Psalms of David, which have been used by almost all composers of religious music.

In some ways, the concept goes back to the *Book of Genesis* and the creation of the world which is beautifully described by Joseph Haydn's late oratorio *The Creation,* in many ways a pastoral symphony with voices. To understand Haydn's oratorio we must be aware that the 'pastor' is God or Christ, looking after the land and sheep and humankind. The 'Lord is my shepherd' concept is very much a pastoral one, and that is why a pastoral symphony like Beethoven's masterpiece is not just a description of nature, but also a praise of the Almighty for having created the world. The best interpretations of this music, like the ones by Karl Bohm and Toscanini, are spiritual.

The purest exposition of the pastoral concept is probably Handel's *Pastoral* Symphony in *Messiah* where music describes the shepherds awaiting and celebrating the coming of Christ. From *Messiah* we get an idea of the classical image of the pastoral as illustrated in paintings. There are shepherds and shepherdesses and sheep, and nature is slightly wild. This is the aura around David in the Bible.

Vivaldi created similar images in *Il Pastor Fido* and *The Four Seasons.* In the pastoral mood created through music, divine and human love exists side by side. In *Il Pastor Fido* or 'the faithful shepherd', Vivaldi, with the help of the flute, the viol and wind instruments, creates the kind of atmosphere that exists in the paintings of Holman Hunt and Boucher. Vivaldi's *The Four Seasons* is also pastoral in mood. In these compositions, he also appears as a poet and creates a dramatic libretto in a series of sonnets that he sets to music.

Haydn is a composer whose rustic simplicity makes him an ideal interpreter of the pastoral mode. *The*

Creation is his tribute to nature and music. Then there is the *Lark* Quartet (op. 64, no. 5) in which he depicts the soaring flight of the bird with the help of the first violin. Shelley's *Skylark* comes to mind, but Haydn's soaring bird is also the human soul with the 'infinite passion' above the 'finite hearts that yearn'. Very few compositions describe the pastoral mood the way this quartet does.

It is very difficult to single out a work that communicates pastoral feelings in Mozart, but his glorious andantes take our minds away from the four walls of a room into the wide open spaces—which is why his music could have therapeutic effect on stressed individuals. Beethoven himself described his famous *Pastoral* Symphony as a description of feelings rather than specific landscape paintings, thereby communicating the total pastoral ambience. But he also composed a beautiful pastoral piano sonata (op. 28) which is like a frozen ode and brings to mind the poetry of the Romantics.

The other day, a young man described Schubert's *Trout* Quintet as music that reminds him of children, but it is quintessentially pastoral in mood, as also are his two piano trios. Not all composers have called their creations 'pastoral', but they have been able to convey the mood, as Dvorak did in his Fifth Symphony, which has one of the most charmingly innocent beginnings since Beethoven's *Pastoral* Symphony. The allegro ma non troppo of the first movement is pure nature, sung to celebrate the sprouting of fresh grass.

Gustav Mahler is another composer who, in two of his works, creates the pastoral ambience—the song-cycle *Das Lied von der Erde,* in which he set a series of Chinese poems on nature to music, much as Vivaldi did in *The Four Seasons,* but with a sense of intense sadness; the other work is the Third Symphony, in which the composer is the true pastor, listening to summer as it marches in—the words of the meadow flowers, the small creatures of the forest, the language of the night and the morning bells, and ultimately equating all this with human love.

Vaughan Williams called his third symphony *Pastoral.* Ironically, it was composed during World War I. The symphony is a series of slow movements, and, towards the close, a wordless soprano fades out. The effect is magical and reminds one of Keats' *Ode to a Nightingale* where the sad voice of Ruth resurfaces. Vaughan Williams returned to the pastoral mood again and again. His Fifth Symphony, and the tone poem *The Lark Ascending,* are as much pastoral as the symphony which he called a pastoral one.

In the present day, listening to pastoral music has become all the more significant because of its therapeutic value. As Browning would say, it helps to catch 'the soul's warmth and arouse the feeling of love more than tongues can speak'.

Chapter 3

Curtain Callers

The Story of Opera

Opera—Divine Madness

Samuel Johnson, the original lexicographer of English, did not like the opera. He thought it was fanciful, irrational and irritatingly confusing. He was right. It is not surprising that Samuel Johnson was anti-opera. The dictionary is rational, logical and precise; the man who invented it could not possibly like a kind of entertainment that was a form of divine madness whose method is even more maddening than its music.

Opera simply means 'a work'. A prosaic title for a form that is exotic; a work of art, one of the strangest that mankind has created. Opera is drama and music caught in an absurd marriage. (Wagner in fact called his operas 'music drama' because he wanted to be different. He had a point because melody was the least important part of his creations whose heart was the orchestra punctuated by the human voice flowing in a stream continuously).

Opera has story, characters, plot (the story and the plot are known as 'libretto') but everything is subservient to the music. And some of the most sublimely beautiful music ever created by man is in the opera.

Opera was born in 1600. At that time there were two basic kinds of music in Europe—church music and court music—music that praised God and music that entertained man. Opera came as a third presence. It had a bit of both. The gods and goddesses it brought down to the stage emerged out of Greek and Roman mythologies and they created havoc (read drama) in the lives of men and women who were kings, queens, princes and great heroes. If the gods were great, the mortals were also larger than life who communicated with spirits, believed in omens and were on a level playing field with gods, goddesses and supernatural beings.

Ordinary mortals had no place in early opera and often the only role they had was to comment on the action as chorus. But soon they joined the opera, changing its course. This happened with Mozart, and later with Puccini.

Below: Scene from an early comic opera. Facing page: Arguably the must prestigious opera venue is the world.

Teatro alla Scala, Milan

From Rossini to Puccini, every great Italian composer has written for The Teatro alla Scala (La Scala). Built in 1778, it was named after the Duchess of Visconti (part of whose name was La Scala) who had founded a church on the site in the 14th century. By the mid-19th century, La Scala was one of the leading opera houses in Europe, setting new standards especially in stage design. In 1920, the theatre came under the artistic direction of Toscanini and it enjoyed its most glorious period. Maria Callas's presence in the 1950s contributed to a revival of long-forgotten bel-canto operas. It seats 3,000, and afficionados claim that the best sound is to be heard in the cheapest seats in the gallery.

Brian Delf

(a) Scara muccio (b) Mezzetino (c) Arlequino. They were the original prototypes of the clown which has remained a favorite character in opera throughout its history.

(a)

(b)

(c)

In the beginning, the human voice was the sole dominating component of opera. But within a few decades musical instruments were added and the man who did this was Claudio Monteverdi (1567-1643), one of the greatest of opera composers. Most of his operas are unfortunately lost. But there are two that have survived—*Coronation of Poppea* on Emperor Nero and the philosopher Seneca who was his tutor, and *Orfeo* based on the legend of Orpheus and Euridice, an immortal story that has inspired many operas down the centuries including two very famous ones *Orpheus and Euridice* by the German composer Christoph Willibald Gluck (1714-1787) and *Orpheus in the Underworld* by the German-French composer Jacques Offenbach.

From the beginning, the human voice was at the centre of opera, in spite of Wagner and his theories, and it was used in a very special way by the composers. First, there were the songs, known in opera language as *arias* which also evolved but was definitely a presence in the early operas. Then there was sung speech, a form of rhetorical disclaiming that in opera language is known as *recitativ*. The third category was that of the 'chorus'. Over the years, the refinements introduced were duets, trios, quartets, quintets, sextets, septets and octets or singing for two to eight voices. But in early opera there were solo singing, choral singing and *recitativs* or sung speech. These categories of human voices have remained and retained their traditional characteristics throughout the history of opera, from Monteverdi to Handel, Handel to Gluck, Gluck to Mozart and from Mozart to Puccini, Verdi and even Wagner.

Although opera is an irrational, crazy, strange and utterly fascinating world of its own, it is governed by certain conventions. These refer to the use of the human voice, tenor, baritone, bass, soprano, contralto or mezzo-soprano, coloratura or high soprano, counter-tenor or high tenor, almost a male soprano. And then there were the 'castratos'. To understand early opera or opera from Monteverdi to Handel, that is from 1600-1759, we must appreciate the phenomenon called the castratis.

The origin of the castratis was in the church. In the 16th and 17th centuries, all churches had their choirs which consisted of the male soprano, mostly boys. In some cases where the boy had special singing talent, the authorities carried out an operation which retained their boyish voices forever. They were castrated and came to be known as castratos who gravitated to opera and sang both male and female roles.

At that time, females were not allowed to sing in the opera. Some of these castratos became very famous, like divas, and made a lot of money, threw tantrums and made composers as important as Handel write operas especially for them. In most cases the boys who were castrated came from very poor families dependent on the church and who gave permission for a small consideration. Over the years the castrati convention has died. Today the operation is banned. In fact, the last of the castratos sang in the Vatican in 1903 and a recording of his voice exists.

What is the difference between the 'castratis' and the 'counter tenors'? Both have a similar high tenor boyish voice but are not the same. The counter tenor, a style and voice very popular today, are men who have achieved the voice through exercises and training. There is no question of any operation and they live a normal life. Today there are a plethora of counter tenors—Andreas Scholl, David Daniels, Drew Minter, Rene Jacob, Michael Chance a trend that was started by the late Alfred Deller who launched the counter tenor revolution soon after World War II which helped the music industry recreate the age of Handel, Vivaldi, Bach, Monteverdi and other Renaissance and Baroque masters.

It is difficult for us to guess what the castrati sounded like. Today the counter tenor fills the part in opera productions. Some operas use boy sopranos and that is probably the closest that we can reach to the flavour of the castrati voice. From the beginning of opera, the tenor voice was always associated with purity, goodness and heroics. The hero was always the tenor except in operas where the part was specially written for the castratis such as Gluck's *Orpheus ed Euridice* and Monteverdi's *Orfeo*. Today, instead of castratis, either counter tenors or mezzo sopranos sing the part.

The tenor is the king of the opera. And has always been so. Composers have written some incredibly difficult parts for the tenor. Take Mozart's *Don Giovanni,* one of the great operas where the baritone is the major role because Don Giovanni is a very complex character, almost an evil force, and the tenor sings the rather timid Don Ottavio in love with the heroine Donna Anna. Don Ottavio's part is so difficult that only great singers can do justice to it, though it is a small part compared

Drawing of the bird-catcher Papageno from Mozart's Magic Flute.

to that of the baritone Don Giovanni. That's why the tenors are in such demand. The 20th century has produced some great tenors. Some of the greatest have been Enrico Caruso (who was also a very good cartoonist), Beniamino Gigli, Franco Corelli, Guiseppe de Stefano, Alfredo Kraus, Carlo Bergonzi, Fritz Wunderlich and the famous three tenors—Luciano Pavarotti, José Carreras and Placido Domingo. The Three Tenors and other tenors of today have become popular because operatic hits, like the songs of Bollywood films, are made popular outside the film and have a life long after the film is forgotten. The Three Tenors have received their phenomenal popularity because they sang together in 1990 in Italy during the Football World Cup. The Three Tenors concept was conceived and numerous recordings were made including one conducted by Zubin Mehta. The Three Tenors in their numerous recordings sang popular songs from various operas including 'Nessun Dorma' from Puccini's *Turandot*. The Three Tenors (Pavarotti is now dead) are ageing, and have broken up but not before they created a cult and left behind a huge legacy of recordings. Other tenors have imitated the concept including a recording with Three Counter Tenors, which shows the popularity of Baroque and Renaissance music. But, surprisingly there has never been a Three Soprano concept although there have been great sopranos like Maria Callas, Renata Tebaldi and Victoria de Los Angeles.

So much for the tenors. Next in importance and for some even more magical is the baritone. In opera, the baritone voice has always stood for complexity, greed,

quel barbaro dov'è... Madamina, il catalogo è questo...
Batti, batti, o bel Masetto, la tua povera Zerlina...
Mi tradì quell'alma ingrata...
Pentiti, cangia vita: è l'ultimo momento!

Facing page and below: A suite of silhouettes showing different characters from Mozart's operas. The silhouette has always been a major art form in illustrating classical music and the composers.

sensuality; in short, for evil. Arguably the most complex role in an opera—that of Mozart's Don Giovanni is sung by a baritone. The Don Juan or the Don Giovanni legend which originated in Spain has given rise to many plays, poems and operas. Mozart's *Don Giovanni* is a man who is at the end of his career as a conqueror of female hearts. He fails with noble women and seduces peasant girls and is pursued by a woman who has escaped from a nunnery. There is also a hint that he might be a homosexual after all and the only true love of his life is his faithful servant Leporello. In trying to conquer a noble woman Donna Anna, Don Giovanni ends up killing her father. The dead and the living meet in the heart of the opera in a graveyard (spine-chilling music by Mozart) and Don Giovanni invites the statue for dinner, which the statue accepts. At the end, the statue drags him to hell but Don Giovanni does not repent. In this, he shows his once brave heart.

Giuseppe Verdi's *Rigoletto* is another great role for the baritone. Rigoletto is the court jester whose daughter, Gilda, the Duke is trying to seduce. The Duke is not a nice guy but because he is of noble birth the role is given to the tenor who sings some of Verdi's most melodious songs including 'Questa o quel-la' and 'La don-na é-mo-bi-le'.

The bass voice is usually used to portray supernatural characters such as the priest in Mozart's *Magic Flute*. Also kings and emperors are usually sung by the bass such as the characters in Verdi's *Don Carlos* and Modest Mussorgysky's *Boris Gudonov*.

The women, once they were allowed to sing in operas, dominated the music stage and created the concept of the diva. What the castratis were in the Baroque Age, the divas or sopranos became in the Romantic Age in the operas of Rossini and Donizetti, Bellini, Verdi and Puccini.

The soprano usually sings the main role, but operas often have more than one soprano. The contralto or mezzo soprano usually sings for the bad women, or the heroine's friends. The coloratura or the florid soprano plays the supernatural characters such as the Queen of the Night in Mozart's *Magic Flute*. During the time of Rossini, Donizetti and Bellini, also known as the 'Bel Canto' or Sweet Song period, the coloratura soprano was in great demand and sang the main role. In today's world, the coloratura tradition lives on through the recordings of Joan Sutherland, Rita Streich, the incomparable Maria Callas, Victoria de Los Angeles, Montserrat Caballé, Gundula Janowitz and the younger generation singers like Cecelia Bartolli and Sumi Jo.

In the beginning, operas used a few instruments, like the trombone which has always signified the supernatural and drums. Then as the opera form evolved over the centuries, more and more instruments like the trumpet and violin were added. Then the overture, which eventually became the symphony, was born and the orchestra became an integral part.

Even then, opera was and still is primarily a vocal form. Handel, Gluck and Mozart used individual instruments with great poetic beauty and atmospherics and showed the way for the Bel Canto composers. Then came Wagner and with him the orchestra (and not the human voice) became the most important component of the drama. Wagner created the leitmotif or the leading motif concept which indicated the characters and ideas like greed, jealousy, anger, fire, storm, decay, journey, sleep, forests, and almost every other nuances of drama were represented by short motifs in the orchestra. The voice often accompanied the orchestra whereas in earlier operas the orchestra accompanied the voice. To a certain extent, Puccini used this concept but he also added the aria or solo songs with a big melody concept that Wagner ignored. Wagner's best melodies like the clarinet motif that ushers in 'Good Friday' in *Parsifal* is given to an instrument. But Wagner retained the *recitativ* or sung speech which is heard throughout his operas. A blend of Wagner and Puccini with a sprinkling of Mozart finds place in the operas of Richard Strauss, a brilliant orchestrator and a masterly opera composer. But innovations in the orchestration notwithstanding opera without a good vocal melody is a non starter. Wagner is an exception that proves the rule.

Almost all great composers have written operas and here is a short list:

Monteverdi: *Orfeo* and *Coronation of Poppea*
Handel: *Julius Caesar* and arias of counter
tenors that include almost all the operas
Mozart: *Idomeneo, The Abduction From
the Seraglio, Marriage of Figaro,
Don Giovanni, Cosi Fan Tutte* and *Magic Flute*
Beethoven: *Fidelio*
Gluck: *Orpheus and Euridice*
Rossini: *Barber of Seville, William Tell*
Donizetti: *Lucia di Lammermoor,
Don Pasquals, Le elisir d'amore*
Bellini: *I Puritani, Norma*
Verdi: *La Traviata, Il Trovatore, Rigoletto,
Falstaff, Otello, Don Carlos*
Wagner: *Tristan and Isolde,
Parsifal, The Ring Tetralogy*
Richard Strauss: *Der Rosenkavalier*
Puccini: *La Bohème, Madama Butterfly,
Tosca* and highlights of famous songs.

The passing away of the charismatic Luciano Pavarotti (1935-2007) turned my thoughts to the tenor voice. The 20th century has produced some very good tenors, starting with Enrico Caruso, who like Pavarotti became a legend in his lifetime. Pavarotti was not only a large man; his larger-than-life image soared far beyond the act of singing, in which he was at his best in the 1960s and 1970s as his recordings show. After 1980, the media, and to a certain extent Pavarotti's own dramatic instincts, turned him into a myth and a cult.

As I have mentioned earlier, in 1990, during the Football World Cup, Pavarotti launched the immensely popular 'The Three Tenors' concept with his arch rival, Placido Domingo, and José Carreras. After that came Elton John, Bono and Pavarotti's Ravi Shankar-like crossover concerts. Indeed, Pavarotti's life became an opera in itself, which made Franco Zefirelli rightly comment that 'there were tenors and then there was Pavarotti.'

In one sense, Pavarotti's efforts can be lauded. The survival of classical music depends as much on

Below: Two scenes from a historical opera of the Italian romantics. Facing page: Norma *by Bellini.*

den 3 april
Lucie (Mlle Jenny Lind)
Se han mig hatar Jag flyr till dig Edgard!!

the connoisseurs as in its ability to come close to the masses. In this process, Pavarotti did more than any other tenor in the history of the voice. Indeed, there are other tenors, Di Stefano, Bergonzi, Kraus, who many consider had better voices but Pavarotti became a cult. In this Pavarotti was like Caruso a household word. The 20th century has seen a grand parade of tenors which has made it 'the century of tenors'.

The tenor voice derives from the Italian ‘tenore’ meaning ‘holding’. Good tenors can hold on to a note, high or low. The voice originated in medieval times where the tenor was the main singer. When opera developed from 1600 onwards, the tenor was replaced for a few centuries by the castratis. After Handel, who favoured the castratis, came Mozart, who favoured the baritone, though in *Idomeneo* he gave the tenor a grand role. (Incidentally, Pavarotti sang this part gloriously.) The tenor, however, has key roles in *Magic Flute* and *The Abduction From The Seraglio.*

There are various kinds of tenor voices. There is the lyric tenor, the best examples being Beniamino Gigli (1890-1957), who had a divine voice, and Fritz Wunderlich (1930-1966), a voice of astounding beauty that was silenced early through an accident. There was also the great Spanish tenor Alfredo Kraus, a voice of such purity that it is difficult to define its elegance and refinement. Then there is the ‘tenor robusto’, a powerful voice. Both Caruso and Pavarotti can be placed in this category. Finally, there is the ‘heldentenor’ or heroic tenor. Pavarotti’s great rival and his exact contemporary, Placido Domingo, comes under this category. Opera enthusiasts will argue till doomsday as to who is greater—Domingo or Pavarotti. But Domingo had an edge over Pavarotti in one area, that is, Wagner; Domingo, at times almost a lyric tenor, has a silkier, soft voice, while Pavarotti was sheer robustness and power. His interpretations of Puccini, Verdi and his favourite, Donizetti, were peerless. It is, in fact, the Bel Canto Trio of Donizetti, Bellini and Rossini who launched the tenor revolution which reached its peak in the 20th century.

There is a very unique relationship between the tenors of the 1950s and 1960s: Bergonzi, Corelli and Giuseppe de Stefano (also three tenors) and the later Pavarotti circle. During the 1950s and 1960s, the phenomenon of media hype was still unknown. Thus, many opera lovers of today will not recall a singer like de Stefano who recorded with the great Maria Callas who, like Pavarotti, became a legend and a myth. There were also Corelli and Bergonzi, splendidly resonant in Verdi and Puccini. Now in their eighties (Corelli is dead), they are all but forgotten. Yet they sang the same mix of opera and Neapolitan songs as the Three Tenors of today. Their High Cs were just as firm and steady, yet they are alive only in the collections of the historically minded.

The same phenomenon took place after Caruso’s passing on. There were singers like Tauber, the monocled German, and Gigli, who refused to be called the second Caruso, saying that he was the first Gigli. There was Jussi Bjorling, the Swedish singer, who has been beautifully described by the vocal specialist Alan Blyth: ‘Nobody might want to choose between Bjorling, Caruso, Gigli, Bergonzi or some of the present day singing

There have been many operas on the theme of Orfeo but Monteverdi's opera, an early edition of which is shown here, is probably the most famous.

greats like Pavarotti and Domingo as the greatest tenor of the century but there is no doubt that Bjorling is up amongst the elect and can be recommended as a model to any aspiring tenor for the nobility of his art which was always based on the verities of tonal beauty, pure line, breath control and sensitive phrasing.'

What about the post-Pavarotti generation? Well, there is Roberto Alagna (b. 1964) who is a wonderful Verdi singer; José Cura, and Ian Bostridge, who specializes in Benjamin Britten. There is also the somewhat controversial blind singer Andrea Bocelli, who possesses an exquisite voice. With the passing on of Pavarotti and the years taking its toll on Domingo, who has branched off into conducting, and José Carreras virtually into retirement, the focus seems to have shifted to counter tenors who are popularizing Baroque and Renaissance operas of Handel, Vivaldi, Claudio Monteverdi and Marc-Antoine Charpentier. One feels that with Pavarotti gone, it is the end of an era. For the new generation, there is much to prove.

L'ORFEO
FAVOLA IN MVSICA
DA CLAVDIO MONTEVERDI
RAPPRESENTATA IN MANTOVA
l'Anno 1607. & nouamente data in luce.
AL SERENISSIMO SIGNOR
D. FRANCESCO GONZAGA
Prencipe di Mantoua, & di Monferato, &c.

In Venetia Appresso Ricciardo Amadino.
M D C IX.

Invitation to Dance

Costume and setting from an early ballet in opera.

Dance

is an integral part of music. Music that is static is dull. The inner harmony of music is movement, an onward rushing pulse. Beethoven's Seventh Symphony is the very apotheosis of dance. It is a dance of the mind and body. The soul dances. In the hands of Beethoven, the scherzo movement is a cosmic dance. This inherent kinetic quality was inseparable with music until the 19th century when a new dance form called the 'ballet' was born. Its origin, however, lies deep in the past.

In the Baroque Age, for instance, the suite was a string of dances. These dances were not for the feet but for the mind. When opera arrived, dance became a part of it. This is particularly true of the French Baroque masters like Jean-Baptiste Lully, Jean-Philippe Rameau and Francois Couperin. Whole segments were devoted to dance in their opera it did not help the story to unfold but the audience enjoyed the spectacular dance.

The grand Baroque suite, such as Bach's Four Orchestral Suites are a garland of dances—courante, bourrée, sarabande, gigue, allemande—which were

An important ingredient of early opera was the dance. It was performed in elaborate costumes with dancers playing a dramatic as well as decorative role.

originally dances from various countries of Europe. Once danced with the feet, they became transformed through the magic of the composer's genius into dances of the mind. You will encounter them sometimes in the classical quartet and sonata movements.

In the grand courts of Louis XIII and Louis IV of France you would have encountered the Académie Royale de la Musique et de la Danse, which created fabulous dance numbers as court entertainment and the form of the ballet which became so popular in the 19th and 20th centuries. Some of the music of these royal court dance numbers has survived and these dance numbers are indeed very beautiful because they were created by composers like Lully and Couperin. These court ballets, for they could be called that as distinct from the stage ballet which developed two hundred years later, were created to celebrate coronations, marriages, war victories, birthdays and so on.

Dance in the classical symphony in the form of the minuet, can be found in Mozart and Haydn. It is usually the third movement of the four movement symphony. It has a smaller dance within the dance called 'trio' where only a few instruments play while the minuet proper is given out by the entire orchestra. The minuet also appears in the string quartet and in the sonata for piano, as also in the piano trio. The minuet developed into the scherzo in the hands of Beethoven which was a sort of divine, intoxicated cosmic dance as exemplified in the Fifth Symphony. After Beethoven, the scherzo was taken up by the romantic composers and gradually the minuet disappeared. The romantic 19th century however, made its greatest contribution

The Firebird *in Stranvinsky's Ballet by Bakst.*

to dance in the form of the ballet which can be described as opera without words; the story unfolding through stylized gestures and music.

There were four creative forces working on the ballet. The first was the composer who created the music, albeit the most crucial force because ballet could not survive in the repertoire without good music. One of the great ballet composers is Tchaikovsky, who used in his ballet scores like *Swan Lake, Sleeping Beauty* and *Nutcracker,* a new kind of dance born in the Romantic Age known as the waltz. The waltz had a separate existence outside the ballet as can be seen in the music of Johann Strauss but in the ballet it was a key factor of its success and popularity.

Tchaikovsky apart, the other great ballet composers have been Igor Stravinsky and Prokofiev, both Russian. Apart from Adolphe Adam's *Giselle* most of the great ballets have come from Russia. Stravinsky's great ballet trilogy—*Firebird, Petrouchka* and *The Rite of Spring*—music that is immensely popular outside the ballet stage, has changed the course of music. All three were produced at the beginning of the 20th century.

The second creative force is the storywriter whose role is more or less the same as the librettist in opera. Most of the ballet stories in the romantic ballet (which includes Stravinsky and Prokofiev) deal with the supernatural, spirits, fairies, strange animals and birds who are transformed as beautiful maidens and who return to their original form, clowns, puppets, dolls, exotic birds, strange rituals *(The Rite of Spring)* and so on.

Rimsky Korzakov's *Scheherazade* based on the *Arabian Nights* story of a woman who tells fascinating

Design by Bakst for Debussy's ballet L'Apres-midi d'un Faune.

stories in order to survive execution by a whimsical sultan is a very good example of a ballet whose story is important. It was originally an orchestral suite and then became a ballet. Who transformed it? The choreographer—the exponent of a creative genre which has been the gift of the ballet to the music world.

The choreographer is the third crucial centre of the ballet, who marries movement to music and one of the greatest who gave birth to the composer Stravinsky and the dancer Vaclav Nijinsky was Sergei Diaghilev, arguably the greatest choreographer of them all. He was at his creative best in the first two decades of the 20th century when his skill as an impressario coordinated between the composer and choreographers like Mikhail Fokine, stage decorators like Leon Bakst, and artists like Marc Chagall and Pablo Picasso to bring to the world a series of great ballets.

The fourth component that has always been a part of opera and ballet includes stage decor and costumes. Bakst, a wonderful artist not so well known, and Picasso have immortalized this aspect of the ballet. Marc Chagall and Salvador Dali are some other artists who have devoted their genius to ballet productions.

After Stravinsky, Prokofiev and Shostakovich, ballet progressively became realistic and the inspiration for this came from America in the works of Aron Copland and Leonard Bernstein whose *West Side Story* is a great ballet. Today romantic and realistic ballets are two separate genres because of the story. The specially trained method of dancing remains but the story has changed from the supernatural to the natural.

The Composers

The Mighty Three

MR. CRESCENDO

Gioachino Rossini is the only great composer who was born in a leap year—on 29 February 1792. During his lifetime, Rossini, who was an exact contemporary of Beethoven, Schubert and Weber, was immensely popular in, of all places, Beethoven's town, Vienna. No other composer in the history of Western music has been as popular during his own lifetime as Rossini.

Rossini is the only composer whose biography has been written by a great writer. I refer to Stendhal's *Life of Rossini,* which makes for highly entertaining reading. In 1824, Stendhal wrote: 'Napoleon is dead, but a new composer has already revealed himself to the world and from Moscow to Naples, from London to Vienna, from Paris to Calcutta, his name is on every tongue.'

In an era when composers were second-class citizens, Rossini was invited by Prince Metternich, the presiding genius of Napoleonic Europe, to participate in the famous Congress of Vienna (October 1822). Metternich wrote: 'I invite the God of Harmony to come to a conference where harmony is so badly needed.'

Rossini was quite possibly the most famous man of his age. But what's his fame like today? In many ways, the last decade has been a remarkable one for this charismatic composer. Certainly, the singer Cecilia Bartoli, has been making Rossini famous again throughout the opera houses of the world. She is highly rated and has performed almost all the Rossini heroines and is considered one of the voices of the decade. Before her, was Marilyn Horne, another great singer and a Rossini specialist. Today, Rossini's *Largo al Factotum* from his opera *The Barber of Seville,* which is based on the same story as Mozart's *The Marriage of Figaro,* is the most famous aria in the world. It has become Rossini's signature tune. It used to be sung by Rossini himself.

Whether you switch on your music at home or in your car, you can smile with the *Largo al Factotum.* It's an utter delight and gets my vote for being the most loveable aria in all opera. Rossini not only smiles through the music, but also had a wonderful sense of humour in real life, the kind of wit that was later attributed to the conductor Thomas Beecham. My favourite Rossini joke is this: after the death of the composer Meyerbeer, his son came to Rossini with a requiem which he had composed for his father. Rossini examined the requiem and then said, 'Would it not

Different characters of Rossini's The Barber of Seville.

Monsieur
Dantan fit jadis la Caricature du Compositeur Pesarese
Aujourd'hui devenu Pianiste de la quatrième Classe il ne
s'oppose pas a ce qu'elle soit Publiée dans votre Journal
G. Rossini
Passy 25 Juin 1867

Facing page: Contemporary cartoon of Rossini. Below: Rossini's funeral.

have been better if it was you who had died and Meyerbeer had composed the requiem!'

Most people will not believe this, but during his lifetime, Rossini was more famous than Beethoven. In fact, he met Beethoven and had a conversation with the great man, which Rossini later recalled in his old age to the young Richard Wagner. According to Rossini, Beethoven admired his operas and told the Italian composer to make more 'Barbers'. How right and perceptive Beethoven was.

Today *The Barber of Seville* remains Rossini's most famous opera.

Beethoven, of course, was not in any way affected by Rossini's popularity quotient in Vienna. But Schubert was. Because the public in Vienna wanted opera and loved Rossini, the young Schubert thought that composing operas would bring him more fame and money. Alas, it didn't. He wasted a lot of time trying to be a Rossini and his operas are all but forgotten.

Much later, like Sibelius who suddenly stopped composing, Rossini quit the opera glitter and, in fact, quit music and settled down to a quiet life in Paris with his second wife till his death in 1868. Someone once asked him why and Rossini replied, 'When I composed *Barber,* tunes chased me. Now I have to chase the tunes. I am old now and I don't have the energy.' Even so, in his old age and retirement, Rossini composed two wonderful religious works, the *Stabat Mater* and the *Little Solemn Mass*. Pundits and purists often dismiss Rossini as musical ice-cream with chocolate sauce. Rossini, who loved ice-cream and good food, would have said that in life and music, feeding the stomach is as important as food for the soul. Considering the fact that Richard Osborne, one of the world's leading Beethoven scholars, is also a Rossini specialist, Rossini must be saying up there, with a twinkle in his eye, 'Well, I have had the last word!'

OF VELVET AND CHANDELIERS—THE WORLD OF VERDI

To try and tell the story of Giuseppe Verdi in a short space is like writing the history of civilization on a matchbox. In operatic terms, the concept of 'highlights' is very popular. Since Verdi is the great master of Italian opera, this could be called the Verdi Highlight. Verdi's life of 80 years spans almost the entire 19th century and just touches the twentieth. He and Wagner were the two great operatic pillars of the century, the early years of which were shared between Rossini, Bellini and Donizetti. But Rossini, although he lived till 1868, had stopped writing opera after the age of 37 (1829). By 1848, Bellini and Donizetti were both dead. So it was left to Verdi to hold high the flag of Italian opera. And how gloriously he did it! His career ran neck-to-neck with Wagner—thank goodness they were poles apart for it is possible to love both Wagner and Verdi, like tea and coffee.

The highlights of Verdi's life are as follows: He was born a peasant, and always remained a peasant at heart. No wonder there is an abundance of folk tunes in his melodies. He was an only son. He lost his wife early, and his two children died, which almost made him give up composing. Although he married a second time

Verdi conducting.

much later in life, he virtually lived the life of a widower. There were hardly any scandals in his life and the only problems he ever created happened whenever he took up an opera (which was all the time), for he would fall severely ill. All his operas were products of his illnesses. Isn't that amazing, considering their freshness? He travelled incessantly to London and Paris and also to America, and was the owner of several villas and dogs. He loved animals and was always thinking of them whenever he travelled, and gave detailed instructions for their care. He loved reading books on literature, particularly Shakespeare, and philosophy. In fact, no other composer has come so close to the spirit of Shakespeare as Verdi has in his operas. Throughout his life, he wanted to set King Lear to music, but it eluded him. However, he managed to write operas on *Macbeth, Otello* and *Falstaff.* Indeed, *Falstaff* was his final masterpiece, the only comic opera he wrote.

Like Beethoven's music, Verdi's can be divided into three periods. The early period includes great choral operas like *Nabucco* and *Ernani,* closing with *Luisa Miller*. Then came the great trilogy—*Rigoletto* (1851), *La Traviata* (1853) and *Il Trovatore* (1853). These three—the 'RTT' trilogy—constituted the turning point of his career. He had created three eternal masterpieces and never looked back—and he was only 40.

Another peak came after quite a few years later with the composition of *Un Ballo in Maschera* (1859), *La Forza del Destino* (1862) and *Don Carlos* (1867), which were like a bridge to Verdi's final period of the *Requiem,* the famous *Aida,* and the Shakespearean operas. Listen also to *Il Trovatore* and *La Traviata,* and you'll be fascinated by the RTT storehouse of melodies. I know of nobody who has not succumbed to the charms of Verdi after listening to these three operas. Two other operas greatly recommended are *Don Carlos* and *Un Ballo in Maschera (The Masked Ball). Don Carlos* has some of the most wonderful songs for low voices in the whole of opera and *Ballo* is like a diamond necklace. The music simply glitters.

Students of literature should find Verdi a subject of special study with his obsession for Shakespeare. There are many who consider *Othello* his greatest opera, but that is a matter of personal taste. Whether you are an admirer of Shakespeare or not, you shouldn't miss the opportunity of listening to *Aida*. It is perhaps the grandest of all operas. There is a special feeling in listening to Verdi. Marble, velvet and glittering chandeliers—these convey the world of Verdi.

While Wagner puts emphasis on the orchestra, Verdi lays equal emphasis on the vocal line. He uses the orchestra more sparingly, but with ominous effect. Verdi's orchestration often reminds one of the opulent paintings of Delacroix—rich in romantic colours, and with a hint of mystery. *Rigoletto* is like experiencing the Renaissance all over again.

But my vote for the most extraordinary of all Verdi compositions goes to his *Requiem,* which many say was his best opera. It is operatic, but also has a terrible beauty. It is a dark, lugubrious work. No wonder every great conductor has recorded it. The 'Lacirimosa' from this requiem is probably the greatest melody Verdi wrote. It is like looking at Michelangelo's *Last Judgement*.

REAL LIFE OPERA

One wonders whether Giacomo Puccini (1858-1924) might have enjoyed his recent popularity, had 'Nessun Dorma'—that song about the sleepless night from Puccini's *Turandot*—not become the signature tune in a World Cup. Sometimes classical music does require strange crutches to support it.

In a recent BBC interview, the cellist Julian Lloyd Webber denounced such crutches saying that classical music had enough strength to stand on its own. All lovers of Puccini would agree with Lloyd Webber, for this delightful composer needs no World Cup to help him gain mass appeal.

Indeed, there is another connection between football and Puccini. You have all heard of the great football 'wave'. Well, the Puccini melody is also like a wave, a great tidal wave of sound and melody that runs through his operas, whether it is 'Che gelida manina' from *La Bohème,* or 'Recondita armonia' from *Tosca* or 'Nessun Dorma' itself, or any of the exquisite arias from *Madama Butterfly*. A Puccini melody is like the famous Katsushika Hokusai's painting, a divine wave of sound. In fact, there are many who feel that Puccini gets by on a single 'Puccini tune'. But there cannot be any doubt that in opera, he is part of the great quartet with Mozart, Wagner and Verdi, and that no other composer has such a high percentage of works currently active.

The turn of a century will always remind opera lovers of Puccini. For it was at the turn of the 20th century—actually, over a period of eight years—that Puccini gave to the world his three great masterpieces,

Giacomo Puccini.

La Bohème (1896), *Tosca* (1900) and *Madama Butterfly* (1904). It is ironical that Puccini, who once walked eighty miles to hear Verdi's *Aida* staged at Pisa—an event that changed his life—should have been the rising star when Verdi's star had stopped shining. Puccini ensured that romantic opera with a dash of realism would have a smooth and logical transition into the 20th century. By the time, he died of throat cancer as a consequence of excessive smoking, leaving *Turandot* unfinished, Puccini had entered the Hall of the Greats thanks to the acceptance and championship of his works by such singers as Caruso (who incidentally drew some fine caricatures of the master), Beniamino, Gigli, Ezio Pinza, Adelina Patti, Lily Pons, Lauritz Melchior, Toti dal Monte, Geraldine Farrar and Dame Nellie Melba, to mention just some of the singers whom Puccini established and who established the composer.

'Nessun Dorma' hit the top-of-the-pop charts and it turned The Three Tenors into pop totems. Why something similar has not happened with the three top sopranos is a mystery. Puccini always fell in love with the women in his operas—Mimi, Tosca and Butterfly—and he created some of the most famous female roles in opera. Yet whoever has heard of 'The Three Sopranos'? Perhaps the public and the critics cannot come to an agreement as to who the top sopranos of the world are. The possibilities are endless but no one seems to agree as to who today can be called a diva.

Puccini's life was recently turned into a film with Placido Domingo in the title role. It was quite a life. It started with Puccini living on soup—the only thing

Below left: A poster of Puccini's Tosca. *Below right: Poster of Verdi's* Aida. *Facing page: Poster of* Turandot.

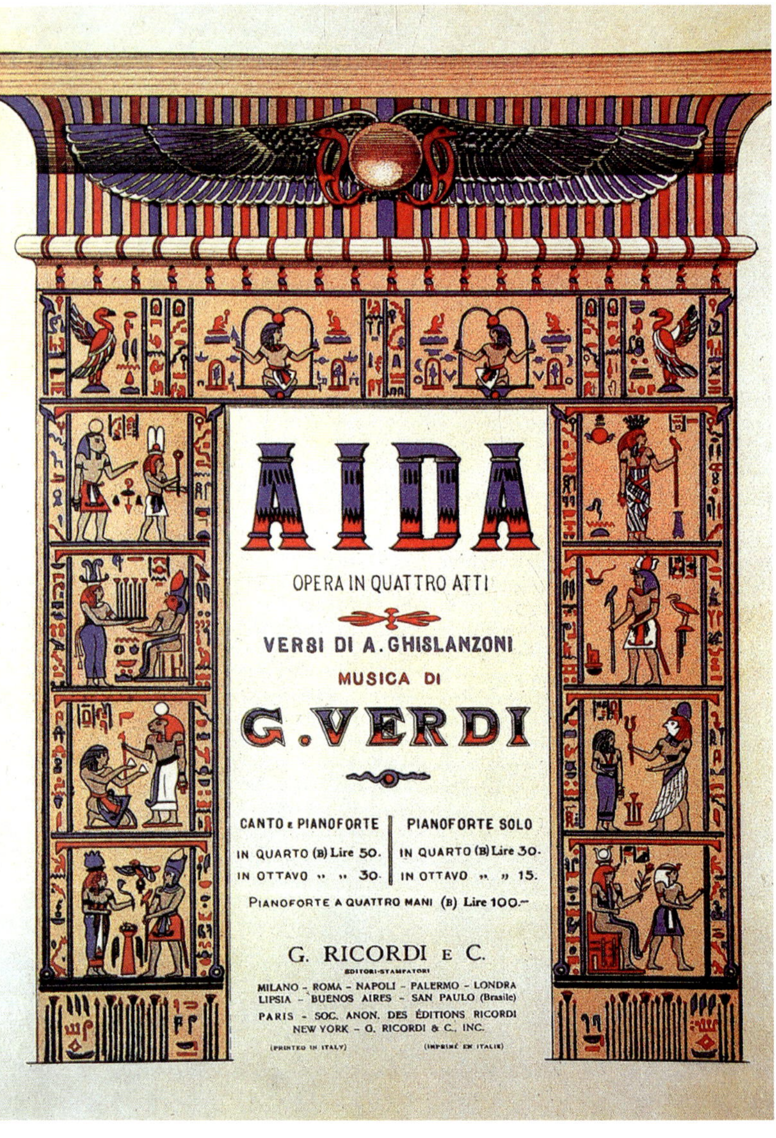

Puccini a cartoon by Carusot.

he could afford to eat—and ended with fast cars, speedboats, horses (it is rumoured that he composed his American opera *The Girl of the Golden West* so that he could put eight horses on the stage), villas, shooting holidays and, of course, women. It is said that it was his early bohemian existence that helped him make *La Bohème* ring so true, and the fact that he loved shooting made him create a lot of violence and blood in *Tosca* and *Turandot,* and in the ending of *Madama Butterfly*.

Puccini, who was fond of writing one-act operas, presents a life which is full of operatic possibilities. Here is a libretto of love. Early in life, Puccini runs away with a married woman named Elvira. For 18 years they cannot marry till Elvira's husband dies. After the marriage, Puccini falls in love with young Doria Manfredi, who is a nurse. Elvira is insanely jealous and tortures the girl till she commits suicide. The Manfredi family is enraged. They order a medical examination which proves that Doria was a virgin. Elvira is sent to jail. Puccini moves towards the most violent of his operas, *Il Tabarro* (The Cloak).

The story behind the composition of *La Bohème* is itself a plot for opera. Puccini, then an unsuccessful composer, is searching for a libretto. He strikes a friendship with another opera composer, Leoncavallo, the composer of the famous *I Pagliacci,* who shows Puccini a libretto—*Scenes of Bohemian Life*—that he is planning to turn into an opera. Puccini, secretly attracted to the libretto, pretends that it is bad, and will only result in a poor opera. His argument convinces Leoncavallo to drop the opera. Puccini quickly composes *La Bohème*. The rest is history.

Dame Nellie Melba as Tosca.

Of course, a shocked Leoncavallo breaks his friendship with Puccini.

The final opera on Puccini's life could be written by an ecologist. Throughout his life, Puccini killed countless birds. He went hunting at night and even indulged in poaching. Every drop of blood shed during Puccini's hunting expeditions returned to take revenge, the, composer contracted throat cancer. He had to undergo many operations, and died coughing blood.

Puccini was the last of the great composers of the romantic opera. With him, the larger-than-life experience of opera came to an end.

FIDDLER PHILOSOPHER

Life was a continuous journey for Yehudi Menuhin (1916-1999), the most mystical of violinists. In the 19th century, virtuoso violinists like Niccolo Paganini reminded people of the Devil; but when Menuhin played, Albert Einstein thought of God. There was a wholesome, healthy optimism about Menuhin which made him win friends and influence people, and made people associate purity and calm with music rather than devilish dexterity.

Appropriately, his end almost coincided with the end of the 20th century. No other musician embodied the musical spirit of the century in its highest essence more than Menuhin and his role in the breaking of musical barriers between the East and West, his fruitful partnerships with jazz violinists like Stephane Grappelli and the sitarist Pandit Ravi Shankar—all contributed to the creation of the concept of a universal music that is typical of the 20th century.

To give just one example of his inspired broadmindedness: some of the greatest classical recordings of this century were made by Menuhin with the conductor Furtwängler. It is a well-known fact that Furtwängler was a pro-Nazi and Menuhin's collaboration with him was criticized by fellow Jews in the United States. For many connoisseurs no greater recordings of Brahms or Beethoven exist. But music for Menuhin was a pure, all-forgiving force that went beyond hatred and revenge. No wonder people associated God and not the Devil with his music. Furtwängler's past was forgotten when they made music.

It is as a recording artist that Menuhin will be remembered by millions across the globe. It is his recorded legacy that will take him into the next centuries. Here, like other 20th century virtuosos Jascha Heifetz, Fritz Krieisler and David Oistrakh, Menuhin scores over his 19th-century counterparts. Menuhin had been recording for about 70 years, and for most of the time on one label—which is some kind of a record.

Everybody knows that he was a child prodigy and as a child his most famous recording is with the composer Edward Elgar conducting his own violin concerto, with Menuhin as the violin soloist. This recording made history and turned Menuhin, then less than 16-years-old, into a celebrity. Amongst historic early Menuhin recordings can be included the one of Bach's double violin concerto he made with his teacher George Enescu, his recordings of Bach and Mozart violin concertos with Enescu conducting, and his 1938 recording of the long-buried Schumann's violin concerto with John Barbirolli and the New York Philharmonic. After Menuhin showed the way, all leading violinists started recording the Schumann Concerto, and now it has become firmly established in the repertoire.

Another composer Menuhin helped to establish is Bela Bartok. In 1943, Menuhin met Bartok and requested him to write a sonata for him. Bartok obliged with a work which Menuhin himself has said is 'one of the most dramatic and fulfilling works that I know of, the most important composition for violin since Bach.' Menuhin recorded the sonata, and the Bartok second violin concerto twice, once with Antal Dorati (a Hungarian like Bartok) and once with Furtwängler.

Menuhin's recording career can be divided into three periods.

The first comprises recordings of him as a virtuoso violinist—he recorded his favourite Beethoven violin concerto thrice, with Wilhelm Furtwängler (1953), Constantin Silvestri (1960) and Otto Klemperer (1966); the other great romantic violin concerto by Brahms, he recorded twice—with Furtwängler in 1949 and Rudolf Kempe in 1957. These are the recordings that will remain the yardstick of his wizardry.

Yehudi Menuhin with conductor Wilhelm Furtwängler.

The second phase of his recording career is associated with his own Bath Festival Chamber Orchestra through which he popularized his favourite Baroque music—Bach, Handel and Vivaldi. It is his Bath Festival recordings that made him a familiar name in India (as also his interest and championship of Indian classical music) with recordings such as the Bach Violin Concertos, Mozart's *Eine Kleine Nachtmusik,* and Haydn's *Farewell* Symphony. The recordings of this unique combination which played a pioneering role in establishing Baroque music in the repertoire also included Handel's *Concerti Grossi* and Bach's *Orchestral* Suites and *Brandenburg* Concertos.

The third phase of his recording career saw Menuhin as a conductor. Like Pablo Casals, Sandor Vegh and more recently, Mitislav Rostropovich, he proved to be a remarkable conductor. According to the reviewer Edward Greenfield, his conducting of the complete Schubert symphonies and Mozart's opera, *The Abduction from the Seraglio,* will remain landmarks. Menuhin also recorded a great deal of chamber music and in this category special mention must be made of his recording of the two Brahms Sextets. Another recording of Menuhin which for a long time has been highly rated by the BBC Record Review is Mozart's Symphony no. 40 in G Minor, performed with the Polish orchestra, the Warsaw Sinfonia, of which Menuhin was the president.

The question as to who is greater, Heifetz or Menuhin, is ultimately as pointless as asking who is the greater tenor, Domingo or Pavarotti. In the Indian context, Menuhin will always have a special niche, not only because of his sympathy with Indian music, or his friendship with Pandit Ravi Shankar, or because Pandit Jawaharlal Nehru attended his concerts, but because Menuhin was ultimately a Renaissance personality much more than just a violinist—he was a humanitarian and a missionary of music. In this, he was much like the other great musician Mendelssohn.

What his favourite composer Mendelssohn did to music in the 19th century by resurrecting Bach from oblivion, Menuhin did for the Baroque master Handel in the 20th century. Incidentally, Menuhin recorded the Mendelssohn Violin Concerto four times. Other recordings by him that many will cherish are the ones he made with the cellist Paul Tortelier and his sister Hephzibah. In fact, Hephzibah and Yehudi became a very popular duo. Menuhin also had a fruitful partnership with Wilhelm Kempff and Louis Kentner.

The term 'music ambassador' is much used today. Menuhin was, in the true sense of the term, an ambassador, not for any particular country but for universal music. Old-timers in Kolkata still talk of his concerts at the New Empire as if they happened yesterday. Others remember him sharing jokes with Pandit Ravi Shankar. Still others cherish his many recordings which introduced them to European classical music. Some quote his pithy sayings and words of spiritual wisdom and talk of the spirit of peace which he emanated.

He was truly the Orpheus of the 20th century.

Chapter 4

Batonability

The Charisma of Karajan

thousand and eight was the birth centenary of that controversial conductor, Herbert von Karajan (1908-1989), who has been extremely well represented in India through recordings ever since he came to this country with the Vienna Philharmonic and was photographed with Pandit Jawaharlal Nehru. From 1960 to 1980, Karajan ruled the rostrum as the most powerful conductor in the world and during those years he had three orchestras under him—the Berlin Philharmonic, the Vienna Philharmonic and the Salzburg Festival Orchestra. Earlier, he began his amazing career by conducting and recording with the Philharmonia Orchestra of London.

The legendary record producer, Walter Legge, who changed classical recording in post-war Europe, spotted Karajan in Vienna. Karajan was then running away from the Allies who had started a search for war criminals in 1946. Legge met Karajan and persuaded him to come to London and begin the most amazing recording career in the history of the gramophone.

Karajan always said that the Berlin Philharmonic and the Vienna Philharmonic were like a wife and a mistress. He was at the helm of both because he wanted to keep them on their toes. The third, the Salzburg Festival Orchestra, came under him for he controlled the Mozart festival in his birth city for more than 20 years. According to Norman Lebrecht in his book *The Maestro Myth,* Karajan modelled his career and attitude on Hitler. He was a card-holding Nazi and till the end, though he denied all charges, he never once spoke against either Hitler or his heinous crimes. There were other conductors—Wilhelm Furtwängler and Karl Bohm—who were linked with the Nazi regime, but Karajan suggested Lebrecht came out the worst in this whole murky affair whose stigma, like a wound that never heals, haunted him throughout his career.

In Israel he could never tour, and the US was always cool towards him. The great impressario Rudolf Bing never hired Karajan for the Metropolitan Opera House. Karajan must share the blame for this dark reputation for he was more a mephisto than a maestro and, what's worse, an incurable megalomaniac. Karajan's incredibly successful career was the result of the most carefully planned image-building process in the history of conducting. He was the complete 20th-century man who had sold his soul to technology, flying his private planes, driving the fastest cars, completely devoted to recordings, and towards the end of his career to films. The fact that he was discovered by a recording genius was like the hour finding the man. Karajan never looked back after the success of his Philharmonia recordings, which were also available in India during the mono LP era. These were his recordings of the Beethoven symphonies, a cycle that he was to record five times in his career, first as monophonic with Philharmonia, the much praised 1962 Berlin cycle and subsequently in 1970 with the same orchestra, then in the 1990s also with Berlin and finally as images on DVD.

Today, some of Karajan's early recordings, like his recording of the Bach B Minor Mass with Kathleen Ferrier, before he became a star are being discovered. Karajan believed that leaving behind recordings was more important than concerts. He would be photographed with eyes closed and arms stretched, as if in a trance, with his sharp Aryan features and handsome presence, like some god of music arriving by mistake at the recording studio.

So fierce was the hatred of Karajan 'the Nazi' in the US that his recordings received strangely contradictory reviews on both sides of the Atlantic. An example is his recording of Mahler's Ninth Symphony which critics in England hailed as the recording of the millennium and was rubbished in New York. Perhaps we should forget Karajan's personal life before passing judgment on his music. He has always been a superb conductor of Rimsky Korzakov, Ravel, Prokofiev, Mahler, Bruckner, Sibelius and Richard Strauss. About Beethoven he received contradictory reviews. His Seventh Symphony and the *Pastoral* have always been highly praised while his first 1962 cycle is regarded as one of the finest of recording achievements in relation to this great composer. His Mozart and Haydn pale into insignificance when compared to conductors of his generation like John Eliot Gardiner and Colin Davis, Karl Bohm and Christopher Hogwood.

Karajan has always been the most reliable conductor for those who are building up a collection. His smooth, silky orchestral sound pleases most people and he is the best guide for entering the world of classical music for the first time. This is why his recordings are such a success. He was called 'Das Wunder Karajan' in the Hitler era and his success has really been miraculous. Hopefully, the years ahead will highlight his achievements without allowing his 'anomalies' as a human being to throw them down to dust.

Of Batons and Bows

On 20 April, 2001, the conductor Giuseppe Sinopoli collapsed and died while conducting Verdi's *Aida* in Berlin. Born in 1946, Sinopoli, a medical man who became a conductor, in many ways symbolized the new generation of young conductors better known for their recordings than for their concepts of performance. Sinopoli, who used to record for Deutsche Grammophon, has left behind a considerable legacy of discs that spans Verdi, Mahler, Puccini Richard Strauss and post World War II, generation of composers. His death in harness has turned my thoughts to conducting, the most remarkable phenomenon of music-making in the 20th century.

The Maestro Myth, which traces the history of conductors in pursuit of power, has few good words to say about conductors, making them appear greedy, manipulating vicious monsters, who also maligned music. But a hundred years later, someone writing a history of music in the 20th century will not be dictated by the jaundiced view that Lebrecht takes, but will surely declare that the trinity of conductors, instrumentalists and singers not only sustained the interest in Western classical music throughout the century, but widened its base and helped resurrect an art form that many considered dead. In the process, conductors like von Karajan, Beecham and Toscanini may have become icons and mythical figures, but there can't be any doubt that Beethoven, Brahms and Mozart, and, more recently, the Baroque and Renaissance composers, owe a debt of gratitude to the breed of communicators called conductors.

The story of conducting in the 20th century actually begins in the 19th century with Hans von Bulow, whose wife Cosima, the daughter of Liszt, ran off with Wagner. Von Bulow established the tradition of conducting Beethoven's charismatic Ninth Symphony. After a brilliant performance of this symphony at Hamburg, von Bulow imperiously silenced the applause. 'Like you, I am also overwhelmed,' he announced, 'I am also touched by your delight in this work of genius.

In accordance with your sincere wishes, I shall perform it again here and now.' When some of the audience made to leave, he requested with exquisite courtesy that they resume their seats. He had, he explained, ordered the exits to be locked. This story, which is probably apocryphal, like most stories about conductors, illustrates the point that I want to emphasize—that conductors have helped to popularize great music.When von Bulow was around, there were no recordings. He was, in fact, doing for the audiences of those days, what recordings do for us today. When we like a work, we play it again and again. That evening at Hamburg, the concept of live recording was born.

Two composers, Gustav Mahler and Richard Strauss, have contributed greatly in developing the phenomenon called conducting. Mahler was a fabulous conductor of opera, particularly Mozart, but he has left behind no recordings. Because of his fame as a conductor, his own music suffered. He heard only a few of his nine symphonies conducted. Today, the yardstick of being considered a great conductor has become the ability to interpret Mahler. Mahler created two great conductors—Bruno Walter and Otto Klemperer, both his pupils, and their interpretations of his many-splendoured symphonies have built his reputation as a composer. That famous duo have been followed by John Barbirolli, von Karajan, Rafael Kubelik, Georg Solti, Claudio Abbado, Bernard Haitink, Zubin Mehta, and, of course, Simon Rattle, the conductor who scored the greatest coup in 2002. Rattle succeeded Abbado by becoming the permanent music director of the Berlin Philharmonic, the first after von Karajan. But none of them have the credentials of Bruno Walter and Klemperer, who actually discussed the symphonies with Mahler. Richard Strauss has left behind quite a few recordings of his conducting, and his operas too have been a breeding ground for conductors like Solti, and later, Sinopoli.

But not all great conductors have become household names. The true fame of a person in any field is when people not particularly interested in the area of specialization, can also immediately recall the name. Arturo Toscanini and Herbert von Karajan are two conductors who have achieved this status. Of course, they belonged to two different generations, but they had one thing in common—a love for Beethoven and a passion for recording. No other conductor, except perhaps Solti, whose recording of Wagner's *Ring* under the late John Culshaw has been voted the greatest recording of the century by the readers of the *Gramophone* magazine, built such a huge legacy of recordings.

Toscanini mostly recorded on 78 rpm, and in a few instances on mono LP. But now, the entire Toscanini collection is available on CD. Von Karajan began with 78 rpm in 1938, then went on from LPs to cassettes and finally CDs and DVDs. Both Toscanini and von Karajan were very camera-conscious, and their photographs on sleeves of the recordings helped people identify them. They almost became monograms of music, and this helped spread their fame. When creative people become household names, myths begin to evolve around them. This has happened with Toscanini and von Karajan. Lebrecht's book on

Toscanini, a cartoon by Caruso.

conductors is an example. But they have propelled music to a new height of popularity that it did not have a hundred years ago.

Another conductor who has become quite a character, and has been the subject of many books, is Thomas Beecham. Beecham jokes are very special, and have sometimes even been compiled on the liner notes of his recordings which have popularized Haydn, Mozart and Delius.

After Mozart's bicentenary in 1956, the conductor's popularity graph soared, reaching dizzying heights in 1991 during the bicentenary of Mozart's death. Beecham was one of the first conductors to give Mozart a boost at a time when not many people knew more of him than *Eine Kleine Nachtmusik*. Beecham also gave a big helping hand to Haydn, the gesture relayed by conductors such as Antal Dorati, Trevor Pinnock and others.

But music-making is serious stuff, and soon after the Beecham era, a new breed of conductors emerged who felt that Beecham's Mozart and Haydn were too romantic. They championed authenticity, and came up with the 'original instruments' concept, which meant making music with the instruments that existed at the time of the composer.

This has been the trend for the last 30 years, and some of the conductors belonging to this school who have become famous are John Eliot Gardiner, Trevor Pinnock, Christopher Hogwood, William Christie, Jordi Savall and Paul McCreesh. They have ushered in the revival of interest in composers like Purcell, Lully, Rameau, Couperin, Scarlatti and Marais.

Lebrecht lists about 150 great conductors. Of these, 90 per cent have left behind a recorded legacy. The choice for the average listener becomes difficult. Some of the legends in the field like Bruno Walter, Otto Klemperer, Arturo Toscanini, Wilhelm Furtwängler and Erich Kleiber, all well known for their interpretations of Beethoven, present no problems. Things begin to get confusing when you are forced to choose between a Sibelius interpretation by Colin Davis or von Karajan, or to opt for an Elgar symphony by Andrew Davis or Georg Solti, or a Brahms by Rudolf Kempe or Claudio Abbado. That is why the era of the faceless conductors, ushered in by the CD boom, and particularly by the budget CD revolution created by Naxos and Point classics is perhaps the best solution. Maybe the time has come when the age of maestros has moved into limbo, and the world of classical music is moving towards a new dawn, where the music is the only hero and the interpreters are as impersonal as the switch of the player. Perhaps it is the only logical way for classical music to survive in the new century.

Conducting: The Electricity in Music

There is a very tragic picture of Beethoven conducting. He was already deaf. Arms are all over and he looks like a wheel of fire, a god drunk with the nectar of music. But we know what happened—because of his tragic deafness, the conducting was absurdly erratic. Yet the audience applauded at the end because the music was like streams of lightning. It was the first time that the Ninth Symphony was being heard by the world. Beethoven could not hear the applause. He only saw it when his friends turned him around to face the audience.

A century later a drunk conductor ruined the career of a composer whose symphony was being inaugurated. The conductor was Alexander Glazunov and the composer was Sergei Rachmaninov. The symphony was Rachmaninov's first. The audience did not take it. Naturally, Glazunov was drunk and hopelessly erratic. Rachmaninov had a nervous breakdown and it is a medical miracle that he could compose again.

I mention these two incidents, one tragic and the other infuriating because I want to underline the key role the conductor plays in bringing music to the world. Today, with the recording boom, the conductor has almost surpassed the composer in importance. People buy a Karajan interpretation or a Klemperer or a Toscanini or a Rattle interpretation. So much so that a newcomer to classical music can ask who is more crucial—the conductor or the composer? The answer is not a simple 'yes' or 'no' but has to be understood in the historical context.

The baton wielding modern conductor directing a huge orchestra like Zubin Mehta or a Claudio Abbado was not born in a day. The electricity of great music has to pass through the conductor to the audience today because the orchestra has grown in size, complexity and dimension.

This was not always so. Conductors have emerged because the forces of music—the orchestra—has grown. In the Baroque Age the conductor was virtually non-existent though not always. The French Baroque composer Jean Baptiste Lully felt it necessary to conduct or direct his

Brahms conducting.

Toscanini conducting.

music, which sometimes included a ballet and opera; large forces which he felt could not be left to the musicians where a double bass would not be able to see a violin or the bassoonist see the cellist and all the singers and dancers. One person had to direct the forces. At first Lully and others like him conducted with a huge stick, like a shepherd's staff or rod with which he would beat and thump the ground. It wasn't a good idea as Lully's case proved. One day at a concert he was so excited that he beat his foot with the stick. The result was that the wound became gangrenous and Lully died. Hundred years later we find the composer Carl Maria von Weber rejecting the Lullyian stick and conducting with a roll rather like the rollers used by marathon runners. The baton as we understand it today evolved from the staff, through the roller. Weber's image, which has been documented, gives a very good clue to the history of conducting. Beethoven in the early years when he was not so deaf used to conduct his own music—a tradition which has remained with composers even today as we find with Dmitri Shostakovich, Vaughan Williams and Edward Elgar. The recording industry has turned these great moments into collector's items. Richard Strauss was a great conductor of Beethoven and his own music. Mahler began his career as a conductor and was not known during his lifetime as a composer.

By the time we come to the early romantics like Weber and Mendelssohn, the necessity and logic of conducting was well established.

But in most cases it was the composer, who logically should know his music best, conducted. Mendelssohn was one of the first composers who began to conduct not just his own music but also that of others like Bach. Such was the electricity of his conducting that the rise of Bach began with the Mendelssohn baton. Mendelssohn conducted London orchestras and also established his own orchestra—The Leipzig Gewandhaus Orchestra—which is even today one of the greatest orchestras of the world. Just when exactly the composer realized that a third party could interpret his music better and that it was good for him to do so because it widened the appeal of the music and popularized it, is not documented. But that was the beginning of the rise of the modern conductor.

Then came Wagner with his gigantic operas which certainly required a sympathetic interpreter and the modern conductor was born in the form of Hans von Bulow who was a great Wagnerite so much so that he gave his wife to him. It is a sordid story but Bulow was a superb interpreter of Wagner and popularized his music. What Bulow did is what all great conductors have done ever since, from Toscanini to Rattle who replaced Karajan as the head of the Berlin Philharmonic. Bulow went into the mind and heart of the composer. He learnt the Wagnerian philosophy and the mystery. He learnt what the composer was trying to say. Then through the orchestra and the singers he created the Wagnerian sound and built the Wagnerian magic.

The conductor is excitingly an interpreter. Today there are the great orchestra conductors who interpret Beethoven, Brahms, Schumann, Bruckner, Mahler, Dvorak, Tchaikovsky, Richard Strauss, and Mahler—all composers who need the full orchestra. Then there is the small orchestra or chamber orchestra conductors who are very good at interpreting Mozart, Haydn and the early classicists.

With the rise of the recording industry and the discovery of the treasures of the Baroque and Renaissance, a third category of conductors have emerged who interpret early music. Early is a dynamic, elastic word when applied to classical music and it can stretch from Monteverdi to Mozart. A special category

A music score.

within this group has become specialists in church music of Giovanni Pierluigi da Palestrina, Thomas Tallis and early religious composers.

Today it is unfashionable to conduct Beethoven the way he was interpreted fifty years ago by conductors like Toscanini, Karajan and Klemperer. A new generation of conductors have emerged who are known as 'original instruments conductors' who study the evolution of musical instruments and try to recreate the sound the composer heard in his time. They say, for instance, that Beecham conducted Mozart and Haydn in an excessive romantic manner with large forces and that these composers must be interpreted with the kind of orchestra that existed in the 18th century.

Yes, conducting and conductors are a very specialized field today and almost all classical music is coming to us through the conductors.

The huge volume of recordings available has also enabled the listener to choose and compare, say, a Toscanini with a Tennstedt, a Walter with a Davis, or a Furtwängler with a Rattle. Ultimately you have to choose a guide. But just remember that the music is more important than the conductor and it is always better to choose the greats—Toscanini, Furtwängler, Walter, Karajan and Beecham. A judicious mixture of the old and the new is what I recommend.

The Inimitable Beecham

The charismatic English conductor Thomas Beecham (1879-1961) is the greatest wit since Oscar Wilde. There are so many Beecham stories that a CD has come out with Beecham at rehearsal where he makes witty remarks. But the Beecham wit hides wisdom as Neville Cardus' biography of Beecham has proved. This book is like an ode and one of the finest tributes that the conductor has received. Cardus' lyrical style makes Beecham come to life.

Many years ago, this book made me fall in love with the conductor and with the music of Frederick Delius, Mendelssohn, Mozart and Haydn—the four composers who have been very closely associated with Beecham. It ends with a wonderful story: 'On his 70th birthday, Beecham was entertained by a great host of admirers. Telegrams and cables from distinguished persons arrived from all over the world. To reverberating applause, the chairman read them out, one after another: 'Congratulations', 'Greetings from Strauss, Stravinsky, Hindemith' and so on, and then finally from Sibelius. And as the cheering died down, Beecham looked up to the chairman from his place at the table and asked with a slightly pained expression on his face: 'Nothing from Mozart?' Cardus concludes the book with a sentence which has always remained etched in my mind: 'Now he lies still and anonymous in Woking cemetery. Woking? Why not Westminster Abbey?'

I went back to the library in search of some more material and found an issue of the *Gramophone* with Beecham on the cover, holding his favourite cigar in his hand and staring at me. I thought of the many times his face had stared at me from LP covers and now CDs. But I recall Beecham's recordings, all on HMV, of 'lollipops'—his coinage for encores—and of Schubert's Symphonies nos. 3 and 5 which he conducted superlatively, Delius, Rimsky Korsakov's *Scheherazade,* and Brahms' Second Symphony, which was also a Beecham favourite.

There is a wonderful story which explains Beecham's attitude to classical and modern music. Beecham had

A cartoon of the conductor Thomas Beecham.

been invited to conduct a programme of Mendelssohn and Stravinsky. The impresario told him: 'I am sure you will require many rehearsals for Stravinsky and none for Mendelssohn.' Beecham replied, 'On the contrary, I require none for Stravinsky, and at least a week of preparation before I conduct the *Italian*.' Beecham was quite naughty at times: 'O.K., start from no. 27—chorus of virgins—you may all sing, ladies.'

At a rehearsal he would often ask, 'What are we playing gentlemen?' One day came the answer: *'The Pathetique.'* 'Let's see what we can do to cheer it up' said Beecham.

After a performance of Vaughan Williams' *Pastoral* Symphony, he murmured, 'A city life for me.' There is a general belief that Beecham was quirky about Beethoven. He would say that his only symphony worth conducting was the Fourth. Yet Beecham was the first to record the great *Missa Solemnis* with Isobel Baillie at the Leeds Festival in 1937.

One of Beecham's finest witticisms is the slightly macabre one about Vaughan Williams and Beecham's pianist wife, both of whom had died. Someone asked, 'How is Betty?' Beecham replied in a flash, 'She is on a tour with Vaughan Williams.'

Cardus once asked Beecham if he was ever at a loss for words. He recalled an incident about rehearsing *Tristan*. He had told Walter Widdop, an intrepid Yorkshireman, to act with more dignity and pride. 'You know who *Tristan* is supposed to be,' said Beecham. And Walter answered, 'E's only a sailor, isn't e?'

Someone once asked Beecham about a composer friend who had passed away. 'Is he still composing?' asked the man. Beecham was rather quick to reply: 'No, he is decomposing.'

Cardus summed up Beecham's achievements by saying: 'He identified himself with the great cause of cheering us all up.' In a world filled with pain and sorrow, it is wonderful to recall Beecham's music-making and his Beechamisms ('The English may not like music, but they love the noise it makes').

Of his recordings, the most outstanding are those of the operas *Carmen* and *La Bohème,* featuring the incomparable soprano Victoria de los Angeles. I grew up with a recording of Handel's *Solomon* which Beecham conducted long before the oratorio became popular, and Haydn's Symphony no. 93. Beecham was also a superb accompanist, and his Sibelius' Violin Concerto with Heifetz is one of the great recordings of the century, as also are his Schubert symphonies and *Messiah*. But above all, Beecham will be associated with the music of Delius, a composer who would have been forgotten but for him. Those, like myself, who love Delius will forever be grateful to Beecham for that.

NOSTALGIA FOR RENAISSANCE

Portrait of Palestrina.

Until the other day I used to think that European classical music began and ended with Bach, then I met my friend Monty Bedi. The complete Renaissance man, he introduced me to Monteverdi and friends Orlando di Lasso, Guillaume Dufay, Josquin des Prez, Giovanni Pierluigi da Palestrina and above all the Abbess Hildegard of Bingen, taking me way beyond the Renaissance into the Middle Ages.

Hildegard (1098-1179), whose fascinating music has been variously described as a 'feather on the breath of God' and 'canticles of ecstasy' has been given the bizarre distinction of being the patron of the American Feminist societies. Whether you are a feminist or not, if you get a chance to listen to the music of this Rhenish aristocrat who joined the Benedictine order, grab it.

I was fascinated too by the music of Guillaume Dufay (1398-1474) and Josquin Des Prez (1440-1521). Dufay's songs had the most flamboyant accompaniment and Josquin wrote music of such strange intensity that I am not surprised that he was Martin Luther's favourite composer.

And then I was haunted by the vision of Don Carlo Gesualdo (16th century) the only composer who got away with murder. Gesualdo's life is the stuff of Italian opera. He murdered his wife, her lover and their child. His music, not surprisingly is intensely dramatic.

But the strangest composer to emerge out of Monty Bedi's hat was Gregorio Allegri, the one-work man. Allegri's *Miserere* or music based on the Fifty-First Psalm of David, is now an all-time favourite, thanks to the CD era. But until Mozart came along, this work was only known to the Papal establishments and was not allowed to be performed outside the Vatican.

Mozart went and heard it once and immediately memorized every bar of the music. He came home and wrote out the work and thus made Allegri known to the wider world.

Portrait of Thomas Tallis.

Cristobal de Morales (1500-1553) is another charmer. He was an exact contemporary of Michelangelo and his music has an instant appeal for modern musicians. Just as there has been an attempt to jazz up Bach, there have been attempts to jazz up Morales as well. In fact, he sounds glorious with saxophone accompaniment.

Tomas Louis de Victoria (1548-1611) is a composer who is paired with a painter. The artist in question? None other than El Greco. Victoria's music is solemn and sublime and seems like musical interpretations of El Greco's art. He wrote a great requiem.

Between Hildegard of Bingen and Bach, the three great composers are Monteverdi, Palestrina and Orlando di Lasso. My vote goes to Giovanni Pierluigi da Palestrina whose music is of such purity and sublimity that it seems almost like angels singing. Palestrina's great work is the *Missa Papae Marcelli* (Pope Marcellus Mass) and it is a landmark in music history. I have mentioned earlier that at the time when the Mass was composed in 1562, the Council of Trent was on the point of banning all choir music from the church. Palestrina as a protest produced his Mass and it was approved by the committee of cardinals who conceded that it was a perfect piece of music and the Pope also heard it and approved of it.

Palestrina you can't miss but there is much that is endearing in the other two. Monteverdi is the great madrigal man creating hundreds of garlands with voices and di Lasso is the master of the Mass. Ravishingly beautiful is sacred music like the 1610 Vespers and the operas: *Orfeo, Coronation of Poppea* and the *Madrigals*.

During the Renaissance, England was particularly rich in composers. The reign of Henry VIII, Mary I and Elizabeth produced Thomas Tallis, William Byrd, Orlando Gibbons, John Bull, John Dowland and Thomas Morley and many more who made the entire country dance to the tune of the lute and the divine harpsichord.

Byrd, for instance, was so highly regarded as a musician that although he was a Catholic under a Protestant ruler, which at the time was quite dangerous, the quality of his music overwhelmed Elizabeth and she forgave him all his Catholic Masses.

But perhaps the last word on the pre-Bach era should be left to Germany's Heinrich Schutz whose 'sacred symphonies' are a class apart in the entire world of music. Schutz's music is pure, haunting and intensely sublime. He came a hundred years before Bach and now most scholars feel that he was the beacon that lit the way for the great Baroque masters.

The Miracle Makers

An early music instrument workshop.

Through Thee I Sing

Music's miracle makers are the instruments of the orchestra. Through them composers create their magical world of sound. Without them the world would be only silence. Yes, the heart and soul of the voice of music are the musical instruments, including the human voice, the greatest instrument of them all.

There was a time when the human voice was the only instrument known to man, and also allowed for music-making. Then man invented musical instruments. Even today, to come close to the human voice is the goal of many instruments, for instance, the flute. In Bellini's opera *La Sonnambula* (The Sleepwalking Girl) the coloratura soprano is accompanied by the flute and often it is hard to recognize when the voice sings and when the flute warbles. Elsewhere in the book I have talked about the human voice. Here we shall discuss the instruments of the orchestra.

The holy trinity of classical music are the three instruments—the cello, the piano and the violin. Together they form what is known as the Piano Trio in which format the composers have written some glorious music. The most beautiful are the ones by Haydn, Mozart, Beethoven, Schubert and Dvorak. As solo instruments they are fabulous too and have given birth to some utterly ravishing music. The violin concerto, the cello concerto and the piano concerto are three great pillars of the classical repertoire. As solo instruments playing on their own without the orchestra, they have helped composers create music of immense depth, spirituality and sublimity like the cello suites of Bach, the violin partitas of Bach, the piano sonatas of Mozart and Beethoven.

It is interesting to note that while both the cello and the violin are crucial components of orchestral music, the piano had no place in the orchestra until the Romantic Age. Even so, except for a few symphonies which use the piano for special effects, the instrument does not appear at all. It is the complete solo instrument and when it does appear with the orchestra, as in the piano concerto, it comes as a

A rare caricature possibly of the Devil playing a windbag.

solo on equal terms with the orchestra, to fight a duel as it were.

The orchestra is the world. Musical instruments are like the people who live in that special world. The orchestra has grown in size over the centuries; the orchestra that Haydn used is not the same as the one used by Wagner or Mahler or Shostakovich. Naturally the Wagnerian orchestra is much larger than the Haydn orchestra, but that does not mean that Wagner is a greater composer than Haydn. The greatness of a composer depends on how well he uses the orchestra and not on its size. The skill and technique of using the orchestral forces is known as orchestration. Beethoven, for instance, in his monumental Fifth Symphony uses a standard orchestra adding four trombones, for the first time in symphonic music, in the last movement. Yet the music sounds like a cosmic upheaval. The genius Haydn in his 'Drum Roll' Symphony uses the drums to open the symphony with an ominous call to attention: mysterious, threatening, spine chilling.

No one had thought of this idea before Haydn.

Like a well-planned city, the orchestra is well structured with musical instruments. There are the strings. This section includes violins (the most important violin player in the orchestra is called its leader and sits on the left of the conductor), violas, cellos and the double bass.

Some orchestral music only uses string instruments. These are called string orchestras. Great Britain has a very good tradition of string orchestral music from Purcell to Benjamin Britten.

Ceremonial trumpets from an early German woodcut.

The string section of the orchestra is the foundation on which orchestral music is built. The beauty of the music depends on how skillfully the composers contrast it with other sections of the orchestra. This contrast is the dynamic heart of music. Mozart is fascinating listening because he knows exactly how to contrast and when to contrast the string section with the woodwinds and the brass.

The wind section consists of some utterly captivating and key instruments. The oldest of them all is the oboe. This instrument existed in the Biblical times and emerged in its present shape through the reeds and rushes from primitive times. Its piercing sound is both sad and sublime depending on how the composer has used it. Bach and Handel, the two great Baroque masters have used the oboe with magical effect.

Next in the wind group comes the bassoon. (Wind instruments are thus called because they come to life with the help of human breath or wind). The bassoon is also a very old instrument. There is an element of mystery and magic associated with it. It is often referred to as the clown of the orchestra because it can sometimes in its low registers produce ungainly, rustic, and even vulgar sounds that can be the cause of laughter. A famous example of this aspect of the bassoon is in Prokofiev's *Peter and the Wolf* where the old grandfather is symbolized by the bassoon.

But the bassoon is also a sad and sorrowful instrument in the hands of a Tchaikovsky or a Sibelius. Great music obeys only one law, the law of the genius who makes it possible.The bassoon is a favourite instrument for literature and there are countless references to it in poetry. In short it is an instrument with quite a personality.

The flute is the quintessential wind instrument and very popular too with composers for use as a concerto instrument and a solo instrument for sonatas. The great J.S. Bach was particularly skilled in the instrument. At that time Prussia was ruled by Frederick the Great who was a flute player and had Quantz, the greatest flute virtuoso of that era as his teacher. Bach once came to the court and Frederick challenged him with a

An allegorical painting of a man playing a bagpipe.

theme which he had improvised and Bach was to create a series of variations on it. Bach then wrote *A Musical Offering*—one of his finest instrumental pieces. The Baroque Age and the Classical Age were particularly rich in flute music. After Mozart, for instance, not many flute concertos have been written and the flute took its place in the wind section of the orchestra.

The flute has several categories. The little flute is known as the piccolo which was used brilliantly by Beethoven in his great *Choral* Symphony right at the close of the world famous 'Joy' theme. Vivaldi wrote piccolo concertos. Then there is the older wooden flute known as the recorder. With the trend today for original instruments, or recreating the sound that the composer knew, Baroque orchestral music is often performed with recorders and not the silver flute, which is the modern standard. There is also some fine recorder music written by Handel.

The clarinet is the youngest member of the wind family. Mozart was primarily responsible for showing the music world how to use the newly invented instrument. His famous symphony in E flat KV543 (no. 39) can almost be called his clarinet symphony, and shows how beautifully he used winds. This music along with his clarinet concerto and clarinet quintet has set the standard for composers who have followed. Carl Maria von Weber and Louis Spohr are two composers who loved using the clarinet in a highly innovative manner.

The brass section is named thus from the material which makes the instruments—shining brass.

The human breath makes the music possible but the instruments are not called wind instruments.

A wood engraving of a procession of musicians.

THE MAYDENHEAD
of the first musicke that
euer was printed for the VIRGINALLS.
COMPOSED
By three famous Masters: William Byrd, Dr: John Bull, & Orlando Gibbons.
Gentilmen of his Maties: most Illustrious Chappell.
Dedicated to all the Masters and Louers of Musick
Ingrauen
by William Hole.
for
DORETHIE EUANS.
Cum
Priuilegio.
Printed at LONDON by G: Lowe and are to be soulde
at his howse in Loathberry

Illustration of the first music printed for the Virginal, an early keyboard instrument.

The trombone is the most fascinating instrument in this group. Its quasi-religious resonances have made composers associate it with religious ceremonies, the spiritual and the supernatural, the eerie and the other-worldly. Mozart is the quintessential example when he uses the trombone to invoke the ghost of the man Don Giovanni has killed. According to Bernard Shaw, it is the most spine-chilling moment in all music. Over the years, composers have used four or more solo trombones to write funeral music and Beethoven wrote this too which was played at his funeral. There are not too many trombone concertos.

The trumpet is the most dazzling of all the brass. It is a Biblical instrument used in the Psalms and in the Book of Daniel and the Revelation. Michelangelo's *Last Judgement* shows angels blowing trumpets; Keats referred to the instrument as 'silver snarling', a brilliant phrase that captures the dazzle of its sound which was used to suggest the beginning of the world and creation by Richard Straus in *Also Sprach Zarathustra*.

The horn is the most romantic of the brass. Its call invokes the Middle Ages, knights, ladies and the atmosphere created by Alfred Tennyson in his unforgettable poem *Lady of Shalott*. Bruckners's symphonies communicate the spirit of enchanted forests, troubadours on horseback with the help of the horn call. Haydn used it magically in his Horn Signal Symphony no. 31.

The tuba is the double bass of the brass section. Its deep voice is at times sad and lugubrious and at times deliciously funny like a baby elephant walking or a child first learning to use the legs. The deep dark brown and black tone of the tuba has been brilliantly used by composers but there are very few tuba concertos. The most famous is the one by Vaughan Williams.

In a very special category falls the harp, also a Biblical instrument that David used to charm Saul who was trying to kill him. It is also used in the Psalms of David. In the orchestra it creates special effects. The best example of it is the music of Mahler. As a solo instrument it fascinated the Baroque composers, Vivaldi, Handel and Bach. But it is Mozart who wrote the last word in a concerto for flute and harp, one of his most fascinating creations.

Drums are also very important. I have already spoken of the Haydn 'Drum Roll' symphony. Beethoven uses drums with brilliance in the second movement of his great *Choral* Symphony. The music of the Danish composer Carl Neilsen is filled with drum beats like heart beats. The other instruments—celeste, tam tam, xylophone, triangles and bells—are for special effects and have no solo status normally. Their use is entirely to create surprise and add body to the sound. These special instruments are being used more and more in music after the Romantic period, though the Baroque composers used them a lot, sometimes including whips.

Two other instruments—the mandolin and lute—have been responsible for many solo concertos, mostly in the highly innovative Baroque period but were sometimes also used by later composers. Mahler used the mandolin in the *Nachtmusik* of his Seventh Symphony where the guitar is also used.

The guitar is perhaps the most unique of all the special effect instruments. There is a huge crop of solo

Below left: Sixteenth-century illustration of a pipe and tabor player. Tabor is an old drum, the pipe is a reed.
Below right: An eighteenth-century drawing of a harpsichordist.

Roman Buccina, a wind instrument rather like the bugle.

guitar composers who have not made a mark with any other instrument. There are plenty of guitar concertos beginning with Vivaldi to the world-famous *Concerto de Aranjuez* by Joaquin Rodrigo makes for fascinating listening. Berlioz is one composer who could not play the piano but was an expert with the guitar. Niccolo Paganini's guitar music is lovely though he is better known for his violin works.

The life and growth of musical instruments have depended on the taste of the composer and the availability of virtuosos. Even great music instruments like the violin, cello and viola needs virtuosos from time to time to excite the imagination of the composer and bring forth new works. This is the life cycle of all instruments and will continue to be so.

Facing page: An antique violin. Below left: Illustrations from an old book on the family of the first violins. Below right: An early illustration of the cello family.

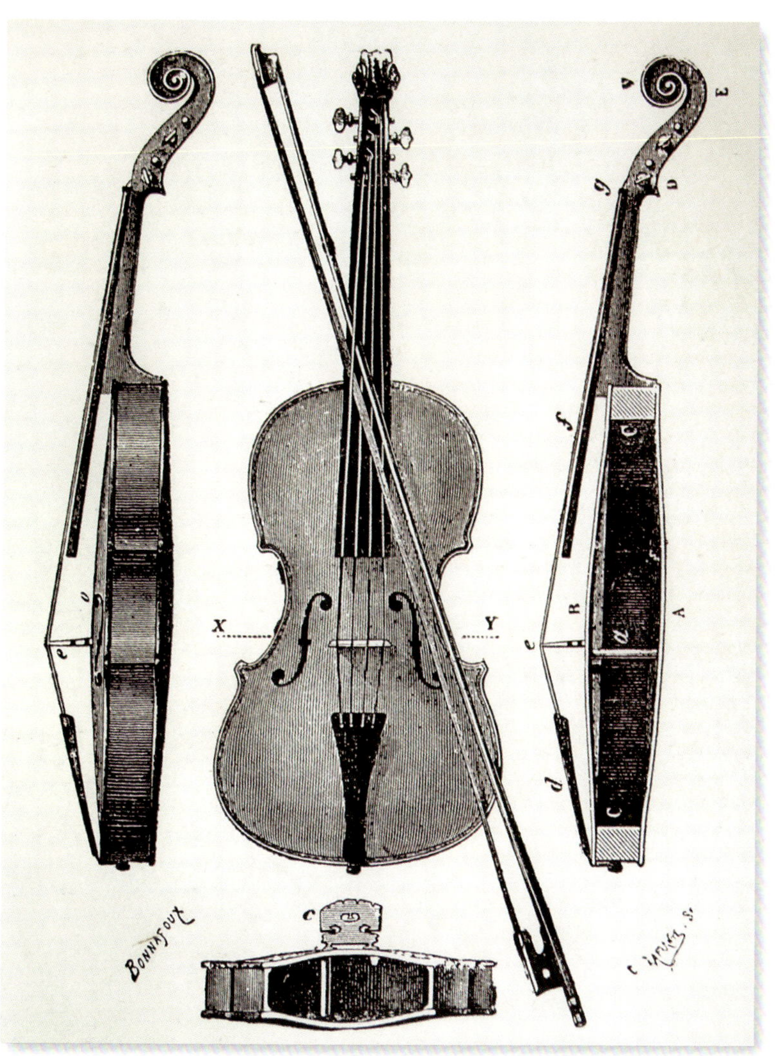

1: 1st violins, 2: 2nd violins, 3: Violas, 4: Cellos, 5: Double basses, 6: Piccolo, 7: Flutes, 8: Oboes, 9: Cor anglais, 10: Clarinets, 11: Bass clarinets, 12: Bassoons, 13: Double bassoon, 14: Harps, 15: Horns, 16: Trumpets, 17: Percussion, 18: Timpani, 19: Trombones, 20: Tubas.

Leader

Conductor

The standard disposition of the modern symphony orchestra is illustrated. Of course, the arrangement will vary from orchestra to orchestra, depending on factors such as the piece being played, the setting, the purpose of the performance and the preferences of the conductor. In addition, a particular symphony may require more or fewer instruments. The key on the right shows the grouping of the instruments by category and name.

By the early 18th century – the era of the master craftsmen of the violin such as Antonio Stradivari – the instrument already had a history stretching back 200 years. Though one or two refinements have since been added (such as the chin rest in 1820), its basic design has proved resistant to major improvements. Foremost in the string family, the violin is the most versatile and has the widest acoustic scope. Its brother, the viola, is similar in design but with a lower range.

The double bass

Early double bass

Three views of the modern double bass

Dating from the early 16th century
double bass has had a chequered hi
going through various five- and six-
phases before arriving at its presen
strings. And for convenience of play
has lost its violin-like shape (top left
gained more steeply sloped should
The 'f holes', too, have varied over th
years. Not until the middle of the 18
century did the orchestra regularly
include the double bass. Now the
symphony orchestra usually employ
eight of them where their combined
lends both force and a basic rhythm
structure. In jazz bands the instrum
played pizzicato: *the strings are plu*
with the fingers rather than bowed,
a symphony orchestra.
Over 200 concertos have been wri
for the double bass and its champio
composers have included Mozart,
Schubert, Strauss, Mahler and Britte

The cor anglais

The cor anglais, otherwise known as the English horn, first made its appearance towards the end of the 17th century. It is the tenor member of the oboe family, and is pitched a fifth lower than the oboe. Its shape varied greatly in its early years – from completely straight, gently curved, to sharply angled. The origins of its distinctive bulb-shaped bell (which it shares with the other larger oboes, the oboe d'amore and the bass oboe) are unknown, and recent research has shown that it does not have a great effect on the instrument's tone. The cor anglais moderne *was made by Brod in 1839, and used a curved crook to hold the reed, in order to overcome the instrument's ungainly length and provide a comfortable playing position. Since then it has undergone major improvements.*

With a rich, deep sound, the cor anglais is generally used for long, slow, plaintive solos, such as in the slow movement of Dvorák's New World Symphony *or Sibelius's* The Swan of Tuonela. *Most professional oboists will possess a cor anglais, though they will not often be asked to play it.*

The oboe

Illustrated below is the modern oboe – separated into its reed plus its three main sections, and assembled. This soprano woodwind instrument, which is made from ebonite, plastic or metal, has 16 to 20 side holes. Of these, six are directly under the player's fingers and the remainder are controlled by intricate mechanisms – a refinement added in the 19th century. The double-reed principle of the oboe, though acoustically very complex and quite difficult for the player to master, is one that can be traced back to ancient history. The characteristic 'reedy' sound has been described as being perhaps the most tender and expressive in all wind music.

The Flute

The flute dates back to the Old Testament and the Ancient Egyptians. The term 'flute', however, covers a wide range of instruments – many bearing little resemblance to the modern flute (below). The modern design is based on a shape devised by Theobold Boehm in 1847; in trying to achieve a greater range of sound the holes were enlarged so much that a mechanical means had to be found to cover them. Boehm achieved this by using a system of rods and pads.

The piccolo (above) is half the size of the flute and is pitched an octave higher. The Boehm mechanical keys were added much later than to the flute. As with the flute the sound is made by the player blowing across the opening, causing the column of air within the instrument to vibrate. The piccolo achieved prominence in the late 18th century and, although it was Beethoven who first included it in major orchestral works – the Fifth and Sixth Symphonies – Tchaikovsky was the composer who provided it with its most splendid orchestral passages.

The bassoon and double bassoon

The bassoon is the tenor and bass woodwind; like the oboe, it has a double reed. Its distinctive double bore, joined at the bottom, gives it a four-octave range and tonal qualities that make it one of the most versatile members of the orchestra. Based on the dulcian, in use before 1700, the instrument designed by Carl Almenräder and J. A. Heckel in Germany in 1843 is the one most commonly used today.

The contra, or double bassoon, uses a larger reed and has a three-fold bore. It excels in the lower register, producing a rich, organ-like sound. Wagner, particularly, encouraged its development and appreciated its virtuosity.

The trumpet

In ancient times the trumpet, used as a military and ceremonial instrument, was a long, straight tube with a flared bell at one end. By the 17th century, this 'natural' trumpet had acquired the much more portable, bent shape it still basically has, and was used extensively by Bach and other Baroque composers. The valves were added in the early 19th century by German makers, greatly improving the instrument's range. The three-valve B flat model is most often used in the orchestra today, although a wide range of higher and lower keyed versions has been developed. Berlioz, in the 1830s, was one of the first to write for the valve trumpet and Mahler, Strauss and Stravinsky went on to compose interesting orchestral parts for it. But only in jazz has it been fully exploited as a solo instrument, most of the current technique being pioneered by Louis Armstrong in the 1920s and 30s.

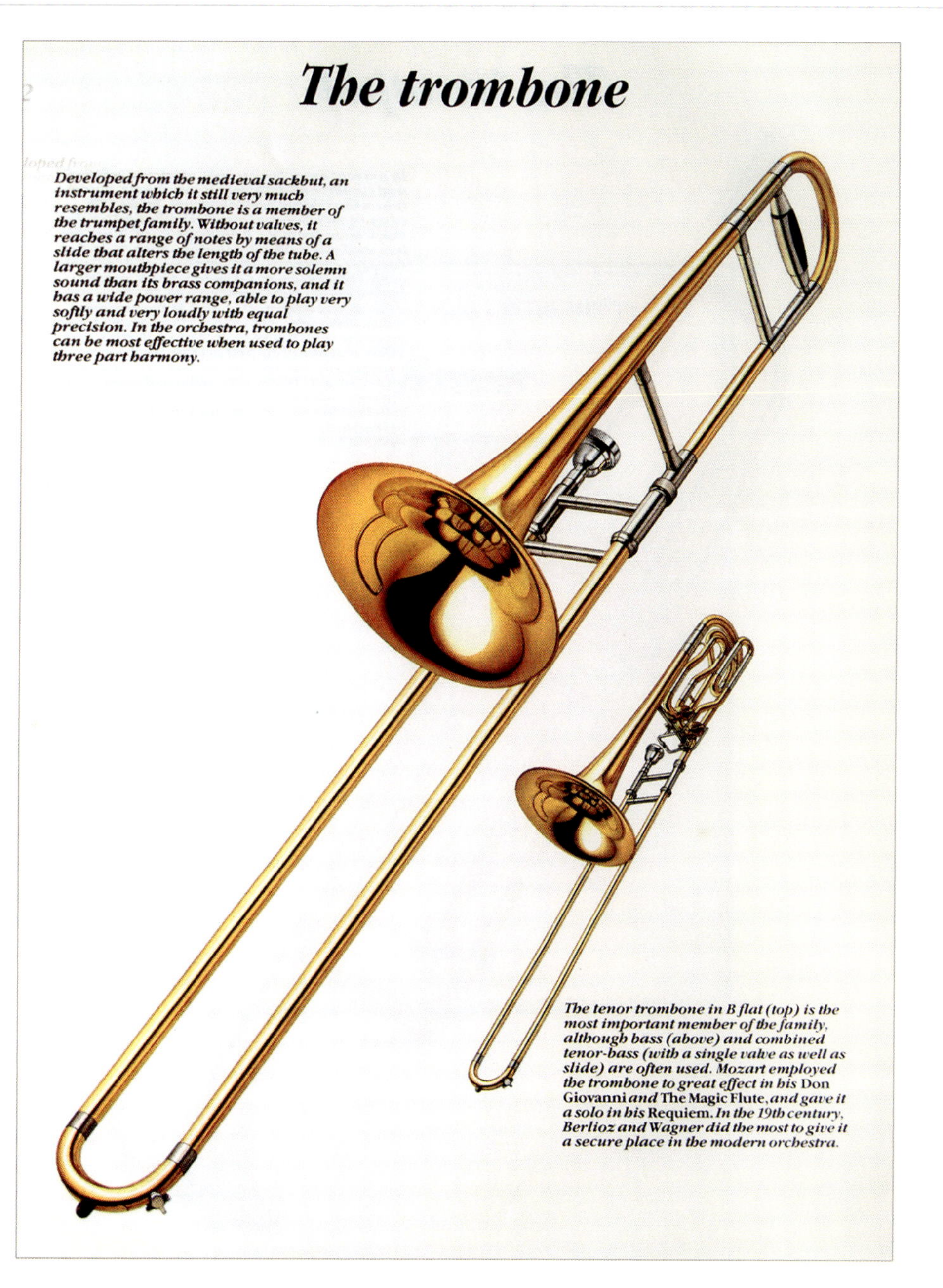

The trombone

Developed from the medieval sackbut, an instrument which it still very much resembles, the trombone is a member of the trumpet family. Without valves, it reaches a range of notes by means of a slide that alters the length of the tube. A larger mouthpiece gives it a more solemn sound than its brass companions, and it has a wide power range, able to play very softly and very loudly with equal precision. In the orchestra, trombones can be most effective when used to play three part harmony.

The tenor trombone in B flat (top) is the most important member of the family, although bass (above) and combined tenor-bass (with a single valve as well as slide) are often used. Mozart employed the trombone to great effect in his Don Giovanni *and* The Magic Flute, *and gave it a solo in his* Requiem. *In the 19th century, Berlioz and Wagner did the most to give it a secure place in the modern orchestra.*

The French horn

The European orchestral, or French, horn is based on early hunting horns first used orchestrally in the early 18th century. Valves, usually three, were added about a century later. Design was revolutionized around 1900 with the development of the B flat/F double horn, now the most common in use. Having a softer, more mellow tone than other brass instruments, horns are often used to sustain harmonies, and act as auxiliaries to the clarinets and bassoons.

In 1849, Schumann became one of the first to compose for the valve horn. Tchaikovsky later gave it an important 'romantic' passage in his 5th Symphony, and Richard Strauss showed its power as a solo instrument.

The tuba

'Tuba' describes any bass-pitched brass instrument that is not a trombone. In their various forms, tubas are descendents of such exotic instruments as the serpent, a kind of bass trumpet with fingerholes, and the ophicleide, a bass bugle with keys.

The first named tuba made its appearance in Germany in 1835. Like all the brass, tubas were vastly improved by the early 19th-century instrument makers. Berlioz, a great lover of brass, was the first to include early tubas in his works, in the 1830s, followed by Wagner who used as many as nine in The Ring, *and Mahler who scored frequent solo passages.*

Today's tubas have from three to six valves (occasionally seven) and produce a massive tone, similar to although heavier than the horn. The tenor tuba in B flat has much the same range as the cello, and is used in the modern orchestra in conjunction with the E flat instrument. Forms of tuba include the euphonium, bombardon, sousaphone and helicon.

The lute and the mandolin

Though no music has been written for it for nearly two centuries now, the lute has the largest repertoire of any instrument, apart from the piano. Several wooden ribs are shaped, bent and glued together individually to form the body while the intricate rose is carved out directly from the soundboard. The very fine gut strings are tuned in pairs, and to prevent the extremely fine soundboard from bending under the tension of the strings, it is supported internally by a series of bars glued to the back which also contribute to the lute's clear, silvery tone. The heyday of the lute was the 16th and 17th centuries, and though Bach wrote four solo suites, almost all the music was composed by lutenists themselves, among whom the Elizabethan, John Dowland, gained unique international fame.

The mandolin, with its several regional variants, was originally indigenous to Italy; but the one we know now is the Neapolitan, whose belly bends down at its widest part. Though similar in appearance to the lute, its artistic contribution is much less impressive. Its eight wire strings are plucked with a plectrum, either with a stroking technique or with the more characteristic repeated sounding or tremolando, which helps sustain its rather insubstantial sound. The soundhole is not quite round and a plate below it protects the wood against the plectrum. Most of its music was written in the 18th century when the mandolin was also incorporated into the orchestra of operas, where it makes its most famous appearance (on stage) in the serenade in Mozart's Don Giovanni.

The harpsichord

Until it was finally superseded by the piano in the mid-18th century, the harpsichord had been the supreme keyboard instrument since the beginning of the 16th century, especially during the Baroque era. There are usually three series, or choirs, of strings and as many jacks as there are choirs, resting on the inner end of each key which plucks the strings. Many harpsichords have two manuals (keyboards): the lower one for sounding all the strings of a note and the upper one, for sounding one string. Stops which protrude from above the manuals operate various mechanisms that affect the tone. Long after its eclipse by the piano, the harpsichord continued to be used in opera as continuo. In spite of its limitations (unknown, of course, at the time), the harpsichord's plangent tones were exploited to the full by Baroque composers, notably François Couperin and Domenico Scarlatti – the greatest of harpsichordists.

Brian Delf

The grand piano
lid
soundboard
frame
bass bridge
main bridge
dampers
strings
keys
Bösendorfer
una corda pedal
sostenuto pedal
sustaining pedal

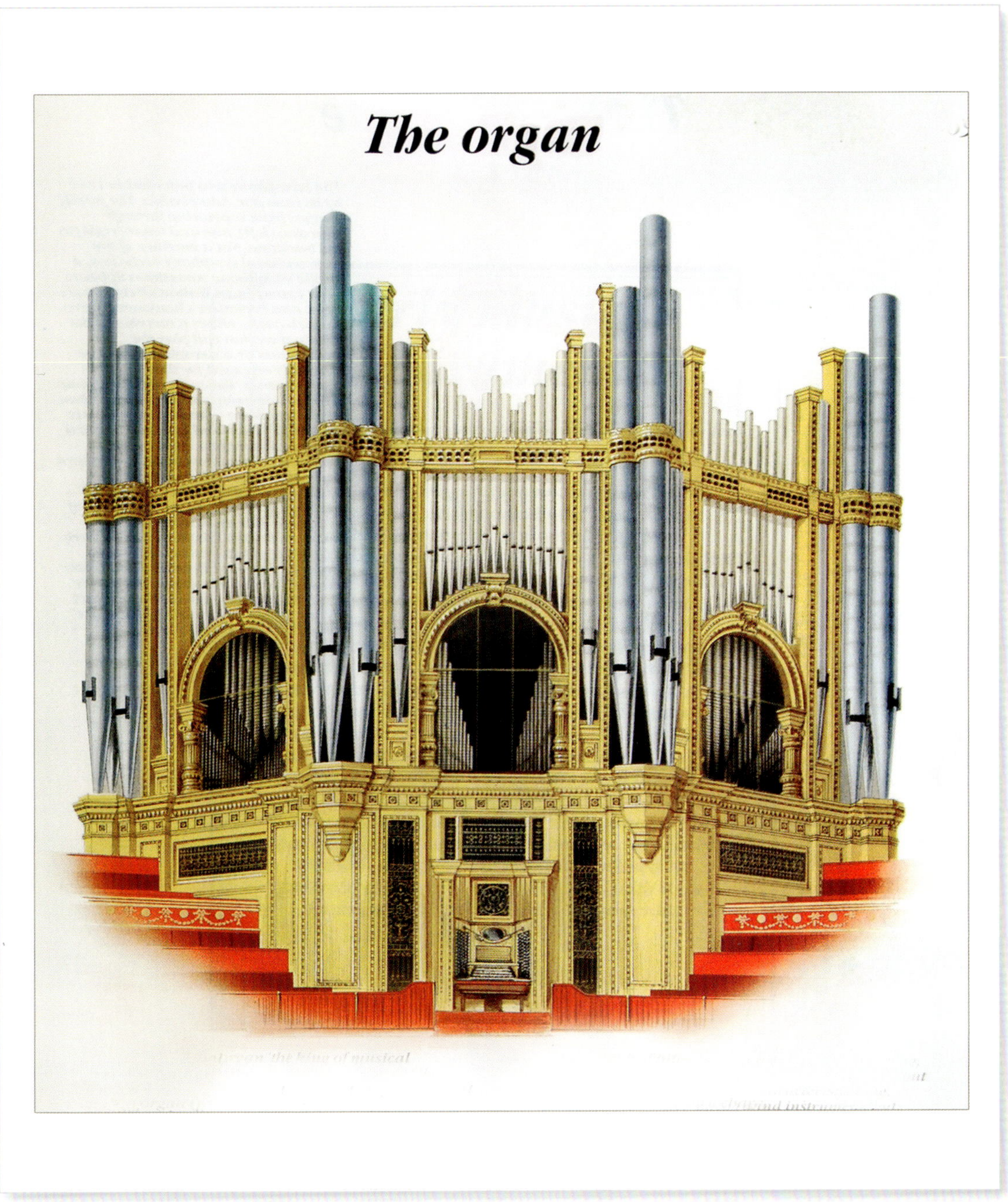
The organ

Epilogue

Creators? Or Interpreters?

How good is the music of the 20th century? How does this century compare with the earlier ones? This is a momentous question and serious music lovers have started pondering on this issue.

To start with, it has been a century in which the taste of the general public proved to be totally different from what the commentators had been saying and advocating. This is a situation which has been unique to the 20th century. For instance, all music books say that two of the most significant path-breaking composers of the modern era have been Arnold Schoenberg and Anton Webern. Yet, ask the man on the street for an opinion, and he would rather listen to Bach, Mozart or even Tchaikovsky. And, yet still, Schoenberg's *Verklarte Nacht* is one of the most beautiful works for string orchestra created after Wagner's *Siegfried Idyll*. Schoenberg and Webern will be remembered for their textbook importance. But who are the composers who will last? First, let us clear the borderline cases, the composers I like to call the leftover romantics—Mahler, Sibelius and Richard Strauss. All these composers were born within five years of each other—Mahler in 1860, Sibelius in 1865 and Strauss in 1864. While Mahler died in 1911, Strauss and Sibelius lived well into the middle of the 20th century. But although Mahler lived only for a little while in this century, yet ironically his best music was written in the last decade of his life.

Therefore, it is important to consider these composers in any discussion on the 20th century's music. Their immense popularity can be considered the result of a yearning for a lost paradise of romanticism in the 20th-century man: the patch of green seen through the stifling mass of grey.

This hankering for the previous century is also seen in the popularity of two composers—both Russian—the brilliant Dmitri Shostakovich and Sergei Rachmaninoff. Both are true composers of the 20th century, yet how shamelessly romantic their music is! Rachmaninoff's poignant Second Piano Concerto is like the heartbeat of the angst-ridden modern man,

New York
2 Febr.
1910.

and Shostakovich's magnificent symphonies carry on the tradition started by Berlioz in the last century, and immortalized by Mahler.

To give just one example, the second movement of Shostakovich's Symphony no. 10, marked allegro, is like corruption set to music. It is the signature tune of the 20th century.

A much-maligned composer who is now justifiably enjoying a worldwide reputation is Edward Elgar. His two symphonies and the Cello Concerto are some of the most moving and pathos-filled pieces composed in the 20th century. Memorable too is the music of Benjamin Britten, particularly the *War Requiem.* No, whenever my mind turns to the modern age, it is not the textbook composers like Schoenberg and Webern that I think of, but Sergey Prokofiev, Carl Orff and even Igor Stravinsky.

Many boys and girls have themselves been introduced to classical music through Prokofiev's *Peter and the Wolf.* Perhaps the statistics will never be known, but this much is certain that Prokofiev can be called the 'Mozart of the 20th Century', with his balance of classicism and romanticism. And of Carl Orff and his ubiquitous *Carmina Burana,* it can be said that like Cesar Franck and his symphony, or Bizet and *Carmen,* he too is fast becoming a one-composition wonder. But what a composition! From advertising commercials to hi-fi demonstrations, *Carmina Burana* is fast becoming the most-played work in modern music. This amazing work for voices and orchestra has had an indirect catalytic effect on musical taste. Composed in 1938 and based on medieval chants, it has since fired an interest in early music.

Although the great divide between critical acclaim and public taste has grown wider, a quartet of composers has built a safe niche in it. They are Claude Debussy, Maurice Ravel, Bela Bartok and Igor Stravinsky. Unlike a composer like Webern, for instance, who has complete textbook importance but hardly any place in public taste, this quartet has kept a balance between text and taste. That is why Stravinsky's three great ballets—*Firebird, Petrouchka* and *The Rite of Spring*—still keep his popularity level high in spite of the so-called importance of his neo-classical music. In *La Mer* and *Bolero,* Debussy and Ravel have respectively contributed two modern masterpieces that are immensely popular, way out of proportion with that of the rest of their output. Their piano and chamber music, especially Ravel's piano concertos, are also beginning to be recognized as treasures worthy of a place with the best that the past centuries have produced. And what of Bartok? Well, the very fact that his string quartets are put in the same bracket as Beethoven's late quartets will make him live forever.

In one way, the 20th century has been musically peculiar. It has not just created its own music but has also promoted the music of past centuries in a way that earlier centuries never have. As the gap between text and taste has grown wider, some of the music of the world that was lost has found a place in it—Gregorian Chants, Monteverdi, Palestrina and even Bach, Vivaldi and Handel. This is not a reflection of the quality of our musical creations but a clear indication

Dmitri Shostakovich.

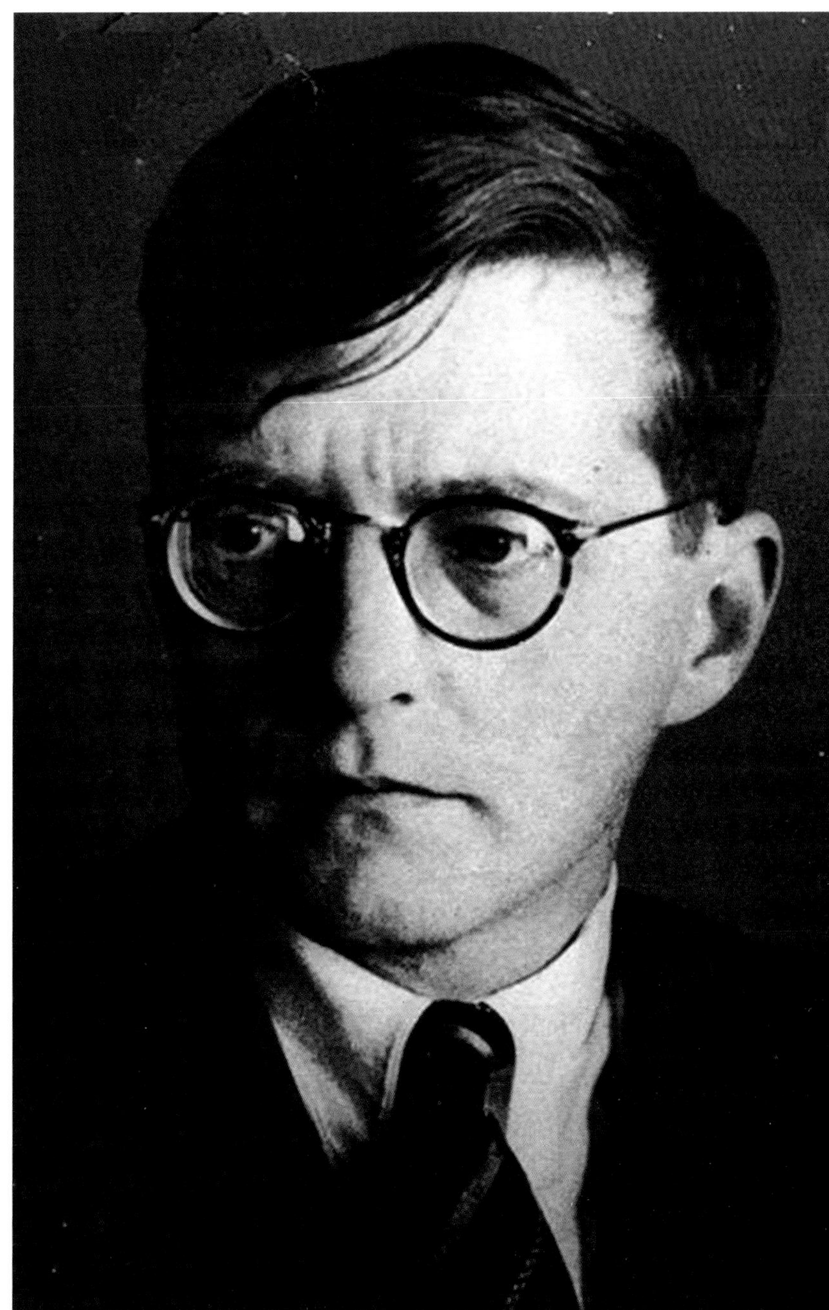

that this century has given more importance to interpretation rather than creation. That is why we have had von Karajans and Toscaninis, Horowitzs and Heifetzs.

But ultimately, people have started to think about who will find a place in the great hall of eternity. Well, if we leave Mahler, Strauss and Sibelius out of this reckoning, for they really belong to the 19th century, my vote will fall on Dmitri Shostakovich as being the most outstanding composer of the century. The power and the glory of his symphonies have strengthened the backbone of classical music which was in danger of collapsing. Shostakovich gave the stream of music new life and new hope.

Beautiful that Batt

There is one book in my music library that I cherish more than any other. This is the 1955 edition of *The Oxford Companion to Music* edited by Percy A. Scholes who founded the original *Companion* first published in 1938. The 1955 edition is a collector's item because of the unique scraper board illustrations of the composers by Oswald Barrett, better known as Batt. Scholes, who was an organist, music critic wrote on music in *The Radio Times* where he met Barrett who also worked there. When Scholes was planning the 1955 edition he asked Batt to illustrate it because he knew that Batt had carried out extensive research on the personal habits of the composers. Oswald Barrett was an ordent music lover and a student of the master musicians. He corresponded with music libraries in Europe and studied visual documents of the composers and their surroundings. Batt also did a colour portrait of Beethoven in which he used well known visual symbols from the composer's life. Beethoven's favourite hat without which he never traveled, is behind him. An ear trumpet can be seen protruding its cone from the chair. Scholes felt it was the most revealing portrait of Beethoven in existence. Batt unfortunately died before the 1955 edition of the *Companion* could be published.

But Batt has lived with me ever since the dictionary entered my collection some 40 years ago. In the first plate Bach is shown studying an organ composition that has just been published. Batt explains in a caption that Bach was primarily an organ composer. It must be noted that it is only after the sixties that the other compositions of Bach was popularized, his cantatas, chamber music, concertos and keyboard works. So Batt can be forgiven for taking a narrow view of Bach. The detail workmanship of Batt's drawing, an amalgam of wood cut and scraper board is mind boggling. The plate on Brahms has conditioned my entire perception of Brahms of a confirmed bachelor with set habits as I saw the picture at an impressionable age. Brahms is shown making a cup of strong coffee. The Handel illustration is brilliant in its execution of details. It shows the composer

Mozart playing billiards. He composed while playing this game. By Batt.

in his old age a blind old man smoking and waiting for the arrival of his amanuensis. His food remains untouched as he has lost his great appetite and his wig hangs from the chair. Mozart at the billiard table is very famous. Mozart compsed musical ideas in his head while playing billiard. Liszt is shown in his old age dressed as an abbe travelling in a coach. Chopin is shown getting down from the coach to attend his last concert. Wagner with an incurable skin disease is shown wrapped in silk. The portrait brings out the feeling of a nasty, hostile personality. Batt was illustrating some 70 years ago and hence there are no picture of Mahler, Bruckner, Sibelius to mention three composers who are very popular now. But Tchaikovsky is there as is Schumann. A few of Batt's paintings is used in this book as a tribute to an unique artist who cut out a very special niche for himself in the would of art and music.

THE HEILIGENSTADT TESTAMENT

(To Karl and Johann van Beethoven)

For my brothers Karl and (Johann) Beethoven

O, you men who believe or declare that I am malevolent, stubborn or misanthropic, how greatly you wrong me! You do not know the secret cause behind the appearance. From childhood onwards, my heart and my mind have tended towards a gentle benevolence. I have always been disposed even to accomplish great deeds. Yet, only consider that for six years I have been suffering an incurable affliction, aggravated by imprudent physicians. Year after year, deceived by the hope of an improvement, finally forced to contemplate the prospect of a lasting illness, whose cure may take years or may even be impossible. Born with a fiery, impulsive temperament, sensible, even, to the distractions of social life, I was yet compelled early in my life to isolate myself, to spend my life in solitude. Even if, at times, I wished to overcome all this, oh, how harshly I was driven back by the doubly grievous experience of my bad hearing, and yet I could not prevail upon myself to say to men: speak louder, shout, for I am deaf. Oh, how could I possibly admit to being defective in the very sense which should have been more highly developed in me than in other men, a sense which once I possessed in its most perfect form, a form as perfect as few in my profession, surely, know or have known in the past. Oh, I cannot do it. Therefore, you must forgive me if you should see me draw back when I would gladly mingle with you. My affliction is all the more painful to me because it leads to such misinterpretations of my conduct. Recreation in human society, refined conversation, mutual effusions of thought are denied to me. Almost quite alone, I may commit myself to social life only as far as the most urgent needs demand. I must live like an exile. When I do venture near some social gathering, I am seized with a burning terror, the fear that I may be placed in the dangerous position of having to reveal my condition. So, too, it has been with me during the past half-year, which I spent in the country. When my reasonable physician ordered me to spare my hearing as much as possible, he almost accorded with my natural disposition, although sometimes, overpowered by the urge to seek society, I disobeyed his orders. But what a humiliation when someone standing next to me heard a flute in the distance and I heard nothing, or when someone heard the shepherd sing and, again, I heard nothing. Such occurrences brought me to the verge of despair. I might easily have put an end to my life. Only one thing, Art, held me back. Oh, it seemed impossible to me to leave this world before I had produced all that I felt capable of producing, and so I prolonged this wretched existence—truly wretched, (because I am cursed with) a body so irritable that a somewhat sudden change can plunge me from the best into the worst of states. Patience—so I am told, it is patience that I must now choose to be my guide: I have patience enough. My determination to hold out, until it pleases the inexorable Fates to cut the thread, shall be a lasting one, I sincerely hope. Perhaps there will be an improvement, perhaps not: I am prepared. Already in my 28th year, I have been compelled to become a philosopher; this is no easy matter, more difficult for an artist than for anyone else. Divine one, thou canst see into my inmost thoughts, thou knowest them; thou knowest that love of my fellow men and the desire

Pg 257: Beethoven, by Batt. Facing page: Part of the Heiligenstadt Testament *written by Beethoven on 6 October 1802.*

to do good are harboured there. O, men, when one day you read these words, reflect that you did me wrong; and let the unhappy man take comfort in his meeting with one of his kind; one who, despite all his natural disabilities yet did everything in his power to be admitted into the ranks of worthy artists and men. You, my brothers Karl and (Johann) as soon as I am dead (if) Professor Schmidt[1] is still alive, ask him in my name to describe my illness, and add this document to his account, so that, as far as possible, the world may be reconciled with me after my death. At the same time, I declare you both to be the heirs to my small fortune (if one can call it such). Divide it fairly, bear with and help each other. The evil you have done me, as you know yourselves, has long been forgiven you. To you, brother Karl, I give special thanks for the devotion shown to me in these recent times. It is my wish that you may lead lives better and more free from cares than my own. Recommend virtue to your children: for virtue alone, not money, can grant us happiness; I speak from experience. It was virtue that raised me up even in my misery; it is owing to virtue, and to my art, that I did not end my life by suicide. Farewell and love each other! I give thanks to all my friends, but especially to Prince Lichnowsky[2] and to Professor Schmidt. I desire that the instruments given to me by Prince Lichnowsky be preserved by one of you; yet let no quarrel arise among you on this account. However, as soon they can be of more use to you in this way, by all means sell them. How glad I am at the thought that even in the grave I may render you some service!

Now it is done. It is with joy that I hasten to meet my death. Should death come before I have had time to develop all my artistic faculties, then, in spite of my cruel fate, it will come too soon and I would wish that its coming might be delayed. Yet even then I shall be content: does not death liberate me from a state of endless suffering? Come whenever it pleases thee to come: bravely I shall come out to meet thee. Farewell and do not quite forget me when I am dead. I have deserved this of you, for often in my lifetime I thought of you, wondering how I could make you happy; be so!

So I must bid you farewell—though sadly. Yes, the cherished hope—which I brought with me when I came here, of being healed at least to a certain degree, must now abandon me entirely. As the leaves of autumn fall and are withered, so, too my hope has dried up. Almost as I was when I came here, I leave again—even the courage which often inspired me on lovely summer days is vanished. O Providence—let a single day of untroubled joy be granted to me! For so long already the resonance of true joy has been unknown to me. O when—O when, Divine one—may I feel it once more in the temple of Nature and of mankind? Never?—no—that would be too hard!

Heiligenstadt, October 6th, 1802.
Ludwig van Beethoven

Beethoven

[1] Johann Adam Schmidt, an eye specialist and Professor of Medicine at Vienna University, who had been treating Beethoven.

[2] He had made Beethoven a present of a set of old string instruments, enough for a string quartet; the makers were Amati and Guarneri.

solche Ereignisse brachten mich nahe an Verzweiflung, es fehlte wenig, und ich endigte selbst mein Leben — nur sie die Kunst, sie hielt mich zurück, ach es dünkte mir unmöglich, die Welt eher zu verlassen, bis ich das alles hervorgebracht, wozu ich mich aufgelegt fühlte, und so fristete ich dieses elende Leben — wahrhaft elend, einen so reizbaren Körper, daß eine etwas schnelle Veränderung mich aus dem besten Zustande in den schlechtesten versetzen kann — Geduld — so heißt es, sie muß ich nun zur Führerin wählen, ich habe es — dauernd hoffe ich soll mein Entschluß seyn, auszuharren, bis es den unerbittlichen Parzen gefällt, den Faden zu brechen, vieleicht gehts besser, vieleicht nicht, ich bin gefaßt — schon in meinem 28 Jahre gezwungen Philosoph zu werden, es ist nicht leicht, für den Künstler schwerer als für irgend jemand — Gottheit du siehst herab auf mein inneres, du kennst es, du weist, daß menschenliebe und neigung zum wohlthun drin hausen, o Menschen, wenn ihr einst dieses leset, so denkt, daß ihr mir unrecht gethan, und der unglückliche, er tröste sich, einen seines gleichen zu finden, der trotz allen Hindernissen der Natur doch noch alles gethan, was in seinem Vermögen stand, um in die Reihe würdiger Künstler und Menschen aufgenommen zu werden — ihr meine Brüder Carl und   , sobald ich tod bin und professor schmid lebt noch, so bittet ihn in meinem Namen, daß er meine Krankheit beschreibe, und dieses hier geschriebene Blatt füget ihr dieser meiner Krankengeschichte bey, damit wenigstens so viel als möglich die Welt nach meinem Tode mit mir versöhnt werde — zugleich erkläre ich euch beyde hier für die Erben des kleinen Vermögens, (wenn man es so nennen kann) theilt es redlich, und vertragt und helft euch einander, was ihr mir zuwider gethan, das wißt ihr, war euch schon längst verziehen, dir Bruder Carl danke ich noch insbesondere für deine in dieser letztern spätern Zeit mir bewiesene Anhänglichkeit, Mein Wunsch ist, daß euch ein bessers sorgenloseres Leben als mir werde, empfehlt euren Kindern Tugend, sie nur allein kann glücklich machen, nicht Geld, ich spreche aus Erfahrung, sie war es, die mich selbst im Elende gehoben, ihr danke ich

Requiem

Requiem (Latin *requies,* 'rest'). The Mass for the Dead, generally sung on All Souls' Day and at funerals and memorial services. It is so called because it begins with the words *'Requiem aeternam dona eis, Domine'* (Give them eternal rest, O Lord).

A Requiem Mass is usually divided into the following sections:

1. *Requiem aeternam dona eis* (Grant them eternal rest)
2. *Kyrie eleison* (Lord, have mercy upon us)
3. *Dies Irae* (The Day of Wrath)
    a. *Dies Irae*
    b. *Tuba mirum* (Hark, the trumpet)
    c. *Liber scriptus* (How the record)
    d. *Quid sum miser* (What affliction)
    e. *Rex tremendae* (King of Glories)
    f. *Recordare* (Ah, remember)
    g. *Ingemisco* (Sadly groaning)
    h. *Confutatis* (From the accursed)
    i. *Lacrimosa* (Ah, what weeping)
4. *Domine Jesu Christe* (Lord Jesus) or *Offertorium*
5. *Sanctus* (Holy, holy, holy)
6. *Agnus Dei* (The Lamb of God)
7. *Lux aeterna* (Light eternal)
8. *Libera me* (Deliver me)

Orlande de Lassus, Victoria, Mozart, Cherubini, Berlioz, Verdi, Dvorak all composed Requiem Masses. The Fauré Requiem omits the *Dies Irae* (The Day of Wrath) and hence it is so peaceful.

Text of the Standard Mass (in Latin and Approximate English Translation)

Kyrie
Lord, have mercy upon us,
Christ, have mercy upon us,
Lord, have mercy upon us.

Gloria
Glory be to God on higher
and on earth peace to men of goodwill,
We praise You, we bless You,
we worship You, we glorify You.

Gratias agimus tibi
We give thanks to You for Your great glory.

Domine Deus
O Lord God, heavenly King, God the Father Almighty.
O Lord, the only begotten Son, Jesus Christ,
O Lord God, Lamb of God, Son of the Father.

Qui tollis
Who takes away the sins of the world, have mercy upon us;
Who takes away the sins of the world, receive our prayer;
Who sits at the right hand of the Father, have mercy upon us.

Quoniam
For You only are holy, You only are the Lord,
You only are most high, O Jesus Christ.

Cum sancto Spiritu
With the Holy Spirit, in the glory of God the Father.
Amen.
Glory be to God on high.
Amen.

Kyrie
Kyrie eleison,
Christe eleison,
Kyrie eleison.

Gloria
Gloria in excelsis Deo
Et in terra pax hominibus bonae voluntatis,
Laudamus te, benedicimus te,
adoramus te, Glorificamus te.

Gratias agimus tibi
Gratias agimus tibi propter magnam glorian tuam.

Domine Deus
Domine Deus, Rex coelestis, Deus Pater omnipotens.
Domine Fili unigenite, Jesu Christe,
Domine Deus, Agnus Dei, Filius Patris.

Qui tollis
Qui tollis peccata mundi, miserere nobis;
Qui tollis peccata mundi, suscipe deprecationem nostrum;
Qui sedes ad dexteram Patris, miserere nobis.

Quoniam
Quoniam tu solus sanctus, tu solus Domimus,
Tu solus altissimus, Jesus Christe.

Cum sancto Spiritu
Cum sancto Spiritu, in gloria Dei Patris.
Amen.
Gloria in excelsis Deo.
Amen.

Credo
I believe in one God the Father Almighty,
Maker of heaven and earth, and of all
things visible and invisible.
I believe in one God.
And in one Lord Jesus Christ,
the only begotten Son of God,
and born of the Father before all ages.
I believe in one God.
God of God, Light of Light, true God of true God,
Begotten not made, consubstantial with the Father.
By whom all things were made.
Who for us men and for our salvation
Came down from Heaven.
I believe.
And was incarnate by the Holy Spirit, out of the Virgin Mary,
And was made man.

Crucifixus
He was crucified also for us under Pontius Pilate.
He suffered and was buried.

Et resurrexit
And the third day He rose again according to the scriptures.
I believe.
And ascended into Heaven, and sits at
the right hand of the Father.
And He shall come again with glory
to judge both the living and the dead.
And His Kingdom shall have no end.
And [I believe] in the Holy Spirit, the Lord and giver of life,
Who proceeds from the
Father and the Son,
Who with the Father and Son together

Credo
Credo in unum Deum Patrem omnipotentem,
factorem coeli et terrae,
visibilum omnium et invisibilium.
Credo in unum Deum.
Et in unum Dominum Jesum Christum,
Filium Dei unigenitum.
Et ex Patre natum ante omnia saecula.
Credo in unum Deum.
Deo de Deo. Lumen de Lumine, Deum verum de Deo vero.
Genitum non factum, consubstantialem Patri,
Per quem omnia facta sunt.
Qui propter nos homines et propter nostrum salutem
descendit de coelis.
Credo.
Et incarnates est de Spiritu sancto ex Maria Virgine,
Et homo factus est.

Crucifixus
Crucifixus etiam pro nobis sub Pontio Pilato.
Passus et sepultus est.

Et resurrexit
Et resurrexit tertia die secundum scripturas.
Credo.
Et ascendit in coelum, sedet ad
dexteram Patris.
Et iterum venturus est cum Gloria
judicare vivos et mortuos.
cujus regni non erit finis.
Et in Spiritum sanctum.
Dominum et vivificantem.
Qui ex Patre Filioque procedit,
Qui cum Patre et Filio simul

is worshipped and glorified,
who spake by the prophets.
And [I believe] in one holy catholic and apostolic church.
I believe.
I confess one baptism for the remission of sins
and I look for the resurrection of the dead.
I believe.
And the life of the world to come.
Amen.
I believe in one God.

Sanctus
Holy, holy, holy, Lord God of Hosts.
Heaven and earth are full of Your glory.
Hosanna in the highest.
Blessed is He who comes in the name of the Lord.
Heaven and earth are full of Your glory.
Hosanna in the highest.

O Salutaris
O saving victim,
who throws open for us the gate of Heaven,
Hostile wars afflict us,
Give strength and bring us help,
Amen.

Agnus Dei
O Lamb of God, who takes away the sins of the world,
have mercy on us
[O Lamb of God] who takes away the sins of the world,
grant us peace.

(Translation © Father David Evans, 1985)

adoratur et glorificatur,
qui locutus est per prophetas.
Et unam sanctam catholicam et apostolicam ecclesiam.
Credo.
Confiteor unum baptisma in remissionem peccatorum
et expecto resurrectionem mortuorum.
Credo.
Et vitam venture saeculi.
Amen.
In unum Deum credo.

Sanctus
Sanctus, sanctus, sanctus, Dominus Deus Sabaoth.
Pleni sunt coeli et terra Gloria tua.
Hosanna in excelsis.
Benedictus qui venit in nominee Domini.
Pleni sunt coeli et terra gloria tua.
Hosanna in excelsis.

O Salutaris
O salutaris hostia,
Que coeli pandis ostium,
bella premunt hostilia,
da robur fer auxilium,
Amen.

Agnus Dei
Agnus Dei, qui tollis peccata mundi,
miserere nobis
[Agnus Dei] qui tollis peccata mundi,
dona nobis pacem.

Essential Classics

Anton Bruckner
Symphony no. 4 'Romantic'

Antonin Dvorak
Cello Concerto
New World Symphony

Antonio Lucio Vivaldi
Four Seasons
Flute Concertos
Oboe Concertos
Cello Concertos
Bassoon Concertos

Benjamin Britten
Young Persons's
Guide to Orchestra

Carl Orff
Carmina Burana

Camille Saint-Saëns
Carnival of Animals

Dmitri Shostakovich
Symphony no. 5

Fryderyk Chopin
Nocturnes
Mazurkas
Piano Concertos

Franz Liszt
Piano Concertos
Piano Music

Felix Mendelssohn
Italian Symphony
Violin Concerto

Franz Schubert
Unfinished Symphony
Trout Quintet

Gustav Mahler
Symphony no. 4

George Frideric Handel
Concerto Grossi
op. 3 and op. 6
Firework Music
Messiah
Organ Concertos
Water Music

Hector Berlioz
Symphony Fantastique
Harold In Italy

Igor Stravinsky
Petrouchka
The Rite of Spring
Firebird

Johannes Brahms
Four Symphonies
Violin Concerto
Piano Concerto

Joseph Haydn
Symphonies nos. 93-104
Trumpet Concerto
Cello Concertos
String Quartet 'Emperor'
Creation

Jean Sibelius
Symphony no. 5
Violin Concerto

Johann Sebastian Bach
Brandenburg Concertos
Christmas Oratorio
Goldberg Variations
Jesu Joy of Man's Desiring (cantata 147)
Orchestral Suites
Suites for unaccompanied cello
Violin Concertos
Keyboard works

Ludwig van Beethoven
Symphonies nos. 1-9
Violin Concerto
Piano Concerto nos. 4 and 5
Piano Sonatas:
Pathetique,Moonlight, Waldstein, Appassionata
Violin Sonata
Spring, Kreutzer

Pyotr Tchaikovsky
Symphonies nos. 4, 5, 6
Piano Concerto no. 1
Violin Concerto
Ballet Music

Rimsky Korzakov
Scheherazade

Robert Schumann
Spring Symphony
Piano Concerto
Piano Music

Richard Strauss
Tone Poems

Sergei Rachmaninov
Piano Concerto no. 2
Symphony no. 3

Sergey Prokofiev
Peter and the Wolf
Piano Concerto no. 5

Wolfgang Amadeus Mozart
Symphonies (nos. 25, 29, 35-41)
Exultate Jubilate
Horn Concertos
Clarinet Concertos
Clarinet Quintet
Marriage of Figaro
Eine Kleine Nachtmusik
Requiem

Popular Western Classical Music Terms

a cappella (Italian)	choral singing without instruments
adagio (Italian)	slow movement, not so slow as largo but slower than andante
adagio assai (Italian)	very slow
adagietto (Italian)	not so slow as adagio, a short adagio composition
affettuoso (Italian)	to play with tenderness and affection
agitato (Italian)	to play in an agitated manner
allegretto (Italian)	moderately quick but not as much as allegro
allegro (Italian)	merry, quick, bright, lively
allemande (French)	a dance found in the Baroque Suite
alto (Italian)	counter tenors are referred to as alto. Also short of contralto. The viola is also referred to as alto
amoroso (Italian)	to play lovingly as in andante amoroso
andante (Italian)	flowing along slow but not too much
andante cantabile (Italian)	flowing and songlike
assai (Italian)	very; Allegro assai: very quick
barcarolle (French)	boat song
bel canto (Italian)	beautiful singing, beautiful song. Refers to singing in the opera of Bellini and Donizetti
berceuse (French)	to rock to sleep. Both Berceuse and Barcarolle are to be found in Chopin and Liszt
bourrée (French)	a dance found in the Baroque Suite very like the gavotte
bravura (Italian)	courage, swagger. A bravura passage calls for brilliant and extrovert display of vocal instrumental technique
brilliante (Italian)	as in allegro brilliante; glittering, sparkling
cadenza (Italian)	a solo passage at the end of the first and last movements of a concerto where the soloist displays his technique without the orchestral accompaniment

cantilena (Italian)	smooth, melodious vocal passage
capella (Italian)	in church style. Vocal writing without instrumental accompaniment
capriccio (Italian)	a composition with unexpected and original effects. Sometimes used with movements of a symphony
cavatina (Italian)	a song like smooth flowing vocal line used to indicate similar movement in instrumental works
chaconne (French)	a dance form with two themes working on two levels also known as passacaglia. Used by Bach and later Brahms
coda (Italian)	The final section of a composition, tail of a work
codetta (Italian)	a little tail. The close of a movement varies. According to composers. The length of a coda on conclusion is variable
col legno (Italian)	striking the wood of string instrument with the stick of the bow. Used by composers for special effects
coloratura (Greek)	a soprano with a voice that can tackle all displays and difficulties as in the arias of *The Queen of the Night* in Mozart's *Magic Flute*
comodo (Italian)	leisurely, gentle without strain
courante (French)	a dance form in the Baroque Suite
da capo (Italian)	repeat from the beginning. Usually applicable to arias in opera, particularly Handelian opera
di molto (Italian)	very much as in allegro di molto or very fast
dolce (Italian)	very sweet with implication of soft
elegie (French)	a song of lament for the dead, same meaning as in literature
equali (Italian)	a quartet of instruments of the same kind usually tuba and trombone. Beethoven wrote equali which was performed at his funeral. Music played at funerals
étude (French)	study. Composition created for the improvement of performance technique. Chopin and Debussy wrote etudes. Schumann and Liszt wrote etudes with fanciful names

fantasia (Italian)	a composition where form is less important than feeling. Very popular with the romantic composers. Fanciful composition that obeys no rules
forte (Italian)	strong, loud
fortissimo (Italian)	strong, very loud
fuoco (Italian)	combination of fire and speed; con fuoco, a combination of force and speed
furia (Italian)	furiously. Fury. Usually referred to as furioso
galliard (Italian)	Lively dance. Baroque suites use it
gavotte (French)	old French dance used in Baroque suites
gigue (Italian)	a lively dance used in Baroque suites
giuseto (Italian)	used with allegro to indicate that it is neither too fast nor too slow. A strict allegro
grave (Italian and French)	slow and solemn. More solemn than adagio
habanera (Cuban)	slow Cuban song and dance. The habanera in Bizet's *Carmen* is famous
harmoniemusik (German)	term used to describe wind music arrangements of opera and symphonies. Mozart used the term
impromptu (French)	term given for improvisation on the spur of the moment. Composition by Schubert Liszt and Chopin
incidental music	music written for creation of atmosphere to accompany action in a play. Beethoven wrote incidental music for Goethe's *Egmont* and Mendelssohn for Shakespeare's *Midsummer Night's Dream.*
intermezzo (Italian, French)	originally used to mean music in the interval of opera. Pergolesi's *La Serva Padrona* was an opera within an opera and is the quintessential intermezzo. In the romantic age it took the meaning of interlude and also a symphonic movement. Brahms and Schumann wrote short piano pieces and called them intermezzi.
invention	name given by Bach to some of his short piano compositions
klavierstucke (German)	short piano pieces
lamento (Italian)	sad and solemn music used by Renaissance composers

landler (German)	a type of slow waltz originating in the landel part of Austria
largo (Italian)	broad slow dignified in style, sometimes very slow. The most famous largo is Handel's song 'Ombra mai fu' from his opera *Serse*
legato (Italian)	bound together, opposite of staccato. Vocal line without pauses
legend (German)	term used for short lyrical compositions. Dvorak and Sibelius used the term
libretto (Italian)	little book. The text of an opera
lied (German)	song. Most famous use is by Schubert. The word comes often in vocal compositions from Schubert to Mahler
lyric	short piano pieces used by Grieg. Not epic or narrative
maestoso (Italian)	majestic, dignified as in allegro maestoso
mazurka	a traditional polish country dance immortalished by Chopin
melody (from German melos)	sometimes used to indicate short pieces as in Dvork
meno (Italian)	less as in meno mosso or less moved or slower
mesto (Italian)	sad, mournful
moderato (Italian)	moderate, restrained as in allegro moderato, bit slower than allegro. Elgar's violin concerto used this tempo
mosso	moved as in piu mosso, more moved
nachtmusik (German)	night music. Chopin used the term 'nocturne' which was invented by John Field. Schubert used the term 'notturno'
obbligato (Italian)	indispensable. Used in chamber music to indicate instruments that can not be dispensed with. Compositions where the composer has marked obligato should not be transcribed
pavane (French)	a form of dance popular in the Baroque era. The dance is solemn and ceremonial at the time of royal mourning
piano (Italian)	soft, quiet, used as an instruction to play softly
	when string instruments are plucked and not bowed

pizzicato (Italian)

poco (Italian)

poem

programme music

quasi (Italian)

recitative (Italian)

rhapsody

riguadon (French)

romance

sarabande (from Spanish Zarabanda)

scherzo

siciliano (Italian)

sordino (Italian)

sostenuto (Italian)

tanto (Italian)

tranquillo (Italian)

troppo (Italian)

woO

a little, indicated in a composition to make the performance loud gradually

literary term used in music by Liszt. A composition with a story. He used the term Symphonic Poem for his narrative compositions

instrumental music that tells story. Not very different from symphonic poems

almost, as if. The most famous example of its use in Beethoven's *Moonlight* Sonata

declamatory speech-like singing in opera

a composition in one continuous movement based on a popular theme or folk melodies

a dance used by Baroque composers

a composition free and fanciful obeying no strict rules. In Italian it is *romanza;* in German *romanaze*. It applies to both vocal and instrumental music

dance form used in the Baroque suite

jest, joke. Monteverdi first used it, Beethoven used it for the movement that replaced the minuet of Haydn and Mozart. Chopin called four of his compositions scherzo

a dance piece of Sicilian origin. Handel used it in *Messiah*. Mozart in a string quartet

a mute for an instrument indicated when the instrument has to put the mutes on

smooth in full flow sustained passage to be played in a slower but sustained speed

too much. Allegro non tanto means don't over do the allegro

tranquilty. To play peacefully

too much. Found in such directions as Allegro ma non troppo fast but not fast

work without opus numbers as in Beethoven's posthumous works

Index